Children's Voices

OF THE SECOND WORLD WAR

HELEN FINCH

FONTHILL

Fonthill Media Language Policy

Fonthill Media publishes in the international English language market. One language edition is published worldwide. As there are minor differences in spelling and presentation, especially with regard to American English and British English, a policy is necessary to define which form of English to use. The Fonthill Policy is to use the form of English native to the author.

Fonthill Media Limited
Fonthill Media LLC
www.fonthillmedia.com
office@fonthillmedia.com

First published in the United Kingdom
and the United States of America 2015

British Library Cataloguing in Publication Data:
A catalogue record for this book is available from the British Library

ISBN 978-1-78155-380-0

Typeset in 10pt on 13pt Minion Pro
Printed and bound by CPI Group (UK) Ltd, Croydon, CR0 4YY

Contents

Acknowledgements

Thank you to all those people who took time to contact me and who feature in this book. Special thanks to the libraries all over the UK who kindly put out my leaflets requesting these stories and whose valuable resources allow everyone access to books like this.

I would like to especially thank my husband Roy, who is patient with me taking so much time up with my writing and also gives a valued opinion. To my two boys, Thomas and Luke, who find this period of history fascinating, especially when their Nanna tells them the stories first-hand.

Special thanks go to my cousin Patricia Lange, who has kindly provided family photographs from her mother, Harriet Lucioni's collection.

Lastly I would like to thank my Mum, Elizabeth, who inspired me to do this publication. If it wasn't for your inquisitive mind and nosiness during your childhood I wouldn't have been told such colourful stories.

Introduction

There have been many books, publications, and programmes mentioning the facts and memories of war. Time is moving fast and soon the memories, if not recorded, will be lost forever.

It is with this in mind that I wanted to record as many of the memories of the children during the Second World War as possible—whether evacuated, stay-at-home, escapees from foreign shores, living abroad or taking in evacuees.

My mother's experiences still fascinate my children and to them, it has a sense of reality, not history. Being evacuated, digging for victory, and rationing seem a bit strange but sound fun. Then she mentions the droning planes darkening the skies, barrage balloons, bomb sites, destruction, and the families torn apart. These descriptions cannot believably be conveyed to those fortunate enough not to have experienced war unless told by the people who were there.

Those children whose memories are included in this publication experienced excitement, danger, sorrow, loss, and adventure. The thoughts of that time live with them today and are just as real to them now as they were during the 1940s. For some, if not all, it shaped their lives, personalities, and the adults they became. One phrase that does stand out is 'times were hard, but we were lucky.'

This book brings together people from all walks of life, each with a story to tell. It has been a pleasure writing and compiling the stories for future generations to appreciate and a shame I couldn't include more. Would the children of the twenty-first century be able to cope with such transitions?

It is seventy-six years since the outbreak of the Second World War, but we must not forget those who sacrificed their lives to enable us to live in peace, both here and abroad. I would also like to remember those brave people who were prepared to put their lives on the line and made it back home to their families, but who are now no longer with us. It should also be remembered that many risked their lives each day on the Home Front to keep Great Britain functioning. They may not have been on the front line, but without their determination our country would have suffered greatly.

I therefore dedicate this book to all those of the Second World War who endured a wartime childhood. We hope nobody will have to see or experience it again. Lest we forget.

Elizabeth Kemble (née Lucioni)

I was born in 1930 in Poplar within the sound of Bow Bells, so I guess I'm a true Londoner. My parents, Walter and Harriet, had already produced a large family: nine children, I being the tenth, then two years later twin boys, so twelve in all. My parents had been brought up in Bethnal Green; they came from poor backgrounds but were honest, hardworking people, and this is what they instilled in us children.

We had moved to Dagenham before the war but then moved to Goodmayes. This house had a front room which we called the parlour and housed the piano. We weren't allowed in this room as it was used for special occasions, but even when we were allowed in, children had to be 'seen but not heard'.

The kitchen was quite roomy and housed a large butler sink. Enough room for a kitchen table and empty orange boxes turned on their sides to be used as bench seats for younger family members. The front of the boxes was used to store our shoes. A copper heated the water and was used on wash day. We had a gas stove and a gas 'geezer' which heated the water for our baths. As this was such a new estate, it afforded such luxuries compared with the last house, which had a hand pump for the water.

The pantry was off the kitchen near the back door, and we were lucky to have an indoor toilet. Steps went down to a large garden which backed onto Goodmayes Park. Luckily for us, there were various types of fruit trees in the garden. We also grew most of our own vegetables. We had chickens, geese, ducks, and rabbits. We all helped in the garden and loved it.

School was great, but when I was in junior school everything changed. It was 1938 and there was talk of a war. Arrangements were made for the evacuation of children. Shelters were supplied to every home. These were made out of corrugated iron and had to be placed in a deep hole which my Dad had to dig in the garden with help from my brother. The other obvious stipulation was that it had to be sited away from the house. Gas masks were delivered to every person in the household, the young children had novelty gas masks, and babies had ones that were similar to a bag and completely covered with an air vent system to allow them to breathe. A lorry would come along to Goodmayes Park and we would have to go in there to be trained to use them. Although they were smelly and made of rubber, we didn't really take much notice and fortunately didn't really need to use them. They were purely a precaution should the Germans drop gas bombs.

The war started on Sunday 3 September 1939. However, many children had already been evacuated on the 1st.

I remember my brothers and sisters saying, 'we want to go away but we don't want a war.' We had our cases already packed, labels to wear round our necks with our names on them, and gas masks in a box. We were fully loaded. Five of us in my family were evacuated. We had to get on coaches from our school to Goodmayes Station. Our parents had to meet us at the station to wave us off. None of the parents had any idea where their children were being taken. It must have been awful for parents just to see their children off at school, then only glance from a distance as they boarded trains. Not even a chance for a cuddle. Luckily for us, my eldest sister Harriet came with us a chaperone. In our group we had two other children for her to look after, a brother and sister whom we knew from school. My Mum had given firm instructions to Harriet, that if we were to be separated she was to bring us home.

Our train took us to a place along the Suffolk coast called Saxmundham. From there we boarded buses to a smaller village called Leiston, where we were all shown into a school hall. The people there then distributed carrier bags with a few bits of food in them, such as an apple and a biscuit. This was to tide us over until we found out where we would be billeted. Some of the local people had already agreed to take children when they arrived.

We weren't so lucky as to have a pre-arranged place to stay, so we had to walk the streets with other children and the helpers knocking on doors to ask whether they had room for us. It was quite exciting and more like an adventure than anything else, as we had other members of the family with us. Yet I'm sure it was upsetting and daunting for the many that were on their own.

Eventually we were the last ones left, but were very lucky to be billeted in a farmhouse that had two additional cottages. Wood Farm was owned by the Snowdons. Predominantly a dairy farm, it also had crops. I remember the cows coming in for milking. Milk would then be put in churns and taken by horse and cart around the village for the locals to collect in jugs. My brother Alf stayed in the cottage with Mr Snowdon Junior and his family. Harriet and my twin brothers, Fred and George, stayed in the farmhouse. Sylvia and I had a bed on what seemed like the landing of the other cottage with the housekeeper. I also recall trying to peer down the stairs once to see what was going on below and falling. We were then moved into a proper bedroom. I was simply living up to my nosey nickname, 'News of the World!'

It was wonderful living on a farm, quite different from the London suburbs. Fresh air, open spaces, and the smells of the country. We would visit nearby Sizewell beach, now known for a nuclear power station. On one occasion my parents came to visit us. As it was early on in the war, the barbed wire hadn't yet been erected along the coast. While sitting on the beach there was a very loud explosion and we witnessed a war ship with its middle dipping into the sea and the ends rising up either side. A torpedo hit. Well that was it. My parents packed up the bags and we immediately left the seaside. Arriving back at the farm my parents explained we were no safer here than near London, so ended our six weeks at Wood Farm. When we left, my twin brothers were given a kitten each to bring home. I don't think my parents were too pleased but the Snowdon's were such nice people I'm sure out of politeness my parents didn't want to upset anyone by saying we didn't really need any more animals.

I revisited the farm when I was eighty years old. It evoked such lovely memories and, surprisingly, I still knew roughly where it was. It was lovely to show my grandsons where I stayed.

School resumed in September 1940, as things were getting back to normal (whatever 'normal' was during the war). Air-raids came mainly during the evenings and at night. We still had lessons but we couldn't waste paper, as it was in short supply.

During the wartime, presents were not as free-flowing as they are today. Clothes would be handmade or we'd get a small gift. So as long as you had meals on the table and were clean and tidy that's all that mattered. We would have family parties, play parlour games, and I remember having indoor fireworks, paper lanterns, and decorations at Christmas. My Mum would stay up all night on Christmas Eve decorating the tree, as it was put up that evening. We would then wake up on Christmas morning and see a beautifully adorned tree with our presents at the bottom. Everyone contributed towards Christmas dinner, from peeling vegetables to Dad carving the meat. The pudding was wrapped in muslin and there would be a silver sixpence inside it. We would all get a chance to stir it when Mum was preparing it and make a wish.

At school we were taught needlework, knitting and other handicrafts, cooking and laundry so we would have skills for the future. Many of my older siblings were in the forces and I was annoyed that I wasn't old enough join up.

My Dad had been in the First World War and had been gassed. He was too old to volunteer into the forces in 1939, as well as being unfit for action. Yet despite working as a milkman in the morning and a newspaper vendor during the day in Bishopsgate, he was an ARP warden for our area. So he was kept very busy. My Mum took over the newspaper stand after he died in 1947.

One funny story I remember during the war was when my brother Alf was working in London. We came home to find a goat in our back garden. He had brought it all the way from the city on the train to join our motley crew of animals. My Mum, although quite sympathetic to an animal's wellbeing, said that it couldn't stay and that he would have to return it from whence it came. She made it up a bed in a shed for a couple of nights until he returned it. In the meantime it would have fun with my twin brothers over the park, where they were seen riding on its back. It must have looked a sight on the train to and from London. Not the sort of thing that would probably be allowed nowadays due to health and safety.

We must have been gluttons for waifs and strays. I recall one time when my eldest brother Walter was on leave from the Army, a man who he'd known from the restaurant where he had been working came to see him. He asked if it was possible that we could look after a monkey, as the woman who owned it had been called up. My mother agreed, so the marmoset monkey came to stay. We had it on a lead indoors as it was very small and it was too cold outside. Eventually we managed to get it a cage to stay in and it was situated in the kitchen. There was, however, a problem with this as the cage was suspended from above and beneath it was where my Dad sat for his meals. Needless to say, there were occasions when he had some of the monkey's food falling into his dinners. My mother then put a shelf above Dad's head to protect his meals. We all loved the monkey, who was a character. He would sit on your shoulder, and his face, hands, and feet were so tiny but perfectly formed. Unfortunately it became ill and although my mother tried to help it, the monkey died. We were all very upset; it had become part of the family.

Another memorable day was when my sister Sylvia was coming home from work and walking over the Ilford railway bridge. Planes were spotted following the train lines and as they came over they started to shoot at the bridge on which she was crossing. She had to dive onto the ground, praying she wouldn't be hit. It left her very exposed.

One Saturday afternoon, my brother Walter had been on leave and was attending the West Ham game at Upton Park. Mum had been shopping with Dad, so they hurried back to the shelter where we had already taken refuge when the air-raid warning had sounded. It wasn't normal for air-raids to be during the afternoon. On this particular Saturday afternoon it was the worst raid. I believe this was the start of the Blitz. The Germans were bombing the docks and you could see the black smoke rising across Dagenham. It wasn't until Walter returned home covered in black soot and muck that he said he had been pulled out of the football match, as he had been wearing his uniform and told to assist wherever possible. It was a very black day.

Life went on during the days of war. We would listen to the wireless and Lord Haw-Haw would frequently be heard with his propaganda speeches. People exchanged food with each other. It was a way of helping each other out and being neighbourly. Fortunately for us we were always stocked up with toilet paper, because my Dad worked on the paper stand. These were old newspapers cut into squares, threaded onto a string, and tied in the toilet. I didn't really think at the time about the print coming off.

The second time we were evacuated it was to my mother's sister in St Albans in Hertfordshire. I believe it was only us younger children who went this time, plus another sister, Ivy. We didn't stay in St Albans long either, and again we came home. As soon as I turned fourteen, I went to work in London.

My first job in the big City was working as a lift operator in a building in Stone House Court near Liverpool Street Station. There were various foreign companies in the building and as all items were on ration, some of them would give me gifts as a thank you for taking them up and down to their offices. Some of gifts were bananas from the Nitrate of Chile and stockings which had three in a pack. This meant that there was a pair and a spare. If my friend who had been given a stocking gift too donated her spare, we were able to give the other girl in another lift the spares so she didn't miss out. Therefore, three of us would end up with a new pair of stockings.

I would travel into London from Goodmayes on the LNER to Liverpool Street Station. It was nicknamed 'Late and Never Early Railway'. It was a steam train and it was usual for us to stand on top of the bridges waiting for the trains to come along and get covered in soot from the funnels. While working in London, I would see POWs being marched through the streets. It turned out that they were Italian.

The raids would often stop the trains. Walking from Liverpool Street to Goodmayes was a frequent event. We weren't allowed to carry lights and so most of this was walking in complete darkness, especially during the winter months, when it was dark not long after we left work. Daylight saving was suspended during the war so the Germans would come over late in the afternoon; this also gave more daylight in the earlier hours, to allow the farmers to work on the fields.

We would walk with people for safety and often stop at Ilford to have a drink at the Milk Bar near to Ilford Hill. This was more than halfway home, but a welcome rest. Sometimes the smog was so bad you couldn't see your hand in front of your nose. I really don't know how we made it home safely. Sometimes we would go off the pavement and go round in circles, ending up where we started.

I remember the celebrations in London when the war ended. There were street parties in our local area, but I also recall the VJ celebrations. The rationing still went on into the 1950s, and I still think people were worried that another war might happen. Growing up during the war is probably one of the reasons why I find sleeping through the night difficult now. I still get up several times and look out of the window.

All shelters were removed after the war and we had to hand in our gas masks. Fortunately we didn't lose any of our family, but my sister had a boyfriend who was killed, though I never met him.

I realise we were very lucky to have our family intact and our home without any damage. War is a terrible experience, but it makes your value what you have and your family around you. My parents did the best they could, keeping our family together, fed, clothed, and cared for. Most of their lives were taken up with two world wars. I think they did a brilliant job and I wish I had the chance to thank them.

Roy Finch

I was born in 1937 in Northfleet, Kent, and during the Second World War was living with my parents and older sister Iris in Bath Street, Gravesend. It was opposite Gravesend Hospital and very close to the River Thames, so I witnessed a lot of action. Most of my memories are of the latter part of the war, from when I was about seven years old.

My parents had made the decision not to evacuate us so we stayed put. I haven't really asked myself why they didn't send us away. We were so close to where the German planes flew along the Thames on their way to and from London. We were also opposite Tilbury Docks, Tilbury Fort, Coalhouse Fort, the airports of Gravesend, and, as the crow flies from Essex, Hornchurch Airfield. We were really in the thick of it. These were all likely targets for German attacks and many a time my friends and I would stand and watch the dog fights taking place over the Thames, Essex, and Hornchurch. I didn't really think of being scared; it was, for us boys, an exciting adventure. It is only as you get older that you realise the extent of what was happening and see things in a different light.

My Dad had been refused entry to the armed forces due to his ulcers, so instead became a member of the Home Guard. When the air-raid warnings sounded and he was out at work, we would make our way round to Nan and Grandad who lived a few streets away. We didn't have an Anderson shelter in our back garden so we would make use of theirs. If Dad was at home then we would go down to sleep in the cellar. He had reinforced it with concrete pillars so it would (hopefully) withstand a blast and we would be safe. I recall taking my gas mask with me everywhere, which at the time was probably a nuisance but a necessary one. We still attended school, but I remember more of the adventures we had around this time than I do that.

My friends and I would always go hunting for shrapnel, and if we found out where a bomb had dropped we would go looking for the bomb sites. The shrapnel would tear your clothes if you placed it in your pockets and cut your hands to pieces, but it was still great to find. We even traded bits of it with each other.

There was a place in Gravesend near to the docks which was known as the 'Undershore'. It was here that they would load and unload the boats, and it wasn't only goods on board. German POWs disembarked from here. They were marched off the boats and we would stand and throw stones at them. Although this was unkind, all we knew was that the Germans were killing our soldiers and, to a child, they weren't very nice. I remember that a lady who lived near us had a German helping her with jobs. After the war they were married and I believe they were ignored by the locals.

Various places were bombed near us. The Food Office at the Prom in Gravesend, where I believe we queued for ration books, was one of them, and the other was the Imperial Paper Mill. It was here that bombs were dropped on the Pulp Yard and we watched for days as the firemen tried to put out the fires.

At Waterdales near Perry Street there was a railway bridge. It was around dinner time, when the children were coming home from school, that a German plane started shooting at the civilians crossing the bridge. I know that the Germans would dump their bombs along the Thames on their way back to the coast, but I don't think this was what they were doing then. There were gun placements which functioned as look-outs over the river at Shorne, which was a little further down, so the enemy could be seen approaching from the coast from near Southend. We would listen for the doodlebug V1s and V2s and when we couldn't hear them we knew they were coming down, and if could see where they were we would run and look for somewhere safe to hide.

I remember watching the iron railings being cut down to be melted down for use in the war effort. They took anything away that was iron and metal.

Although we didn't have a shelter as I mentioned before, we were quite self-sufficient. We had chickens and rabbits and grew our own vegetables. Mum would sometimes send me down to the shops with the ration coupons and I would have to queue up. We didn't have eggs but used egg powder, which I found disgusting. If you had an apple at Christmas you were very lucky. Clothes were also hard to come by and you were lucky if you had a pair of boots. We didn't have toys and would make our own four-wheeled barrows if we were able to get the wheels and wood. My friends and I would also go swimming at Town Pier at high water. I would climb on the top of the ferry pier roof and dive off into the water. Although my Mum thought we were going to the swimming pool, she would always smell my costume when I got home and I always wondered why. 'You've been swimming in the river again,' she would say to me.

Although some of my relatives were in the Army, a few of my uncles worked on the Thames as watermen and lightermen, and also on the river tugs and coal barges. The coal would be taken up to the cement works and to other places along the river. Some of the tugs stayed to move the barges, but others were used in the D-Day Landings. My uncles who were the watermen didn't go to help with D-Day, but stayed to keep the river moving.

The estuary was a very active place, even around as far as Chatham on the River Medway. Chatham Dockyard was very active, housing a submarine base and war ships which came into the dockyard to be repaired. The larger ships couldn't come up any further because they were too big. It was due to my love of the Thames and the waterways and probably because I was living alongside it and watching all that went on that, at sixteen, I became an apprentice waterman and lighterman. I was very proud to get my badge, as it was gruelling work and it takes many years to achieve this. My Dad wanted me to be an electrician, but I'm pleased I went with my own idea.

When the war ended there were lots of parties, and we had one in our street. I can't remember much of it, but I think there was a big one in Gravesend organised by Forrests, who owned the fair that still travels around the area today.

Maureen Timby

I was born in 1935, so was four years old when war was declared. I lived with my brother, who was six years older than me and our parents. My younger sister was born during the war in 1942, and my youngest wasn't born until war was over. We lived in Maple Road on the King's Farm Estate, near Gravesend Aerodrome.

There was an air-raid shelter at the end of the garden. Many a night we would have to run down the garden to the shelter to avoid the bombs dropping all around us. It was very damp and smelly and we would take food down there to eat. Sometimes we would go down our neighbour's shelter. To keep us occupied we would sing and this would help to drown out the noise of the bombs and aircraft. We were very near to the Thames where the planes would come up to London.

I remember a rather large aunt who couldn't get into the shelter so she had to stay indoors under the Morrison shelter. When we came out of the shelter we would look around to see what houses had been hit and whether our home was safe. My Dad was an ARP warden, so wasn't always around during the air-raids. I remember him wearing his armband. He wouldn't let us be evacuated, but I recall a bomb dropping on our friends home in Cedar Avenue. There were also bombs dropping near the General Gordon Hotel. We would go along there for a sing-a-long on a Saturday morning with our friends. The bomb dropped on the sports hall near the hotel, but luckily not on it.

In about 1942 when I was six or seven, I remember a bomb dropping near Whitehill School, Sun Lane, where I was a pupil. The school was five minutes' walk from our house. If we were out and about to and from school and the sirens went we would run into people's houses and share their shelters until the all-clear sounded. People were very kind to us all.

I remember one time very clearly was when I was about eight years old. We were in the CO-OP in Central Avenue and there was such a loud bang. We were all crying and comforting each other. The bomb had dropped at Echo Square, Old Road East. It was only five minutes from us. Everything shook and rattled. We were all scared, not knowing exactly where the bomb had dropped and if anyone was injured.

At night there were search lights everywhere. I used to have very bad nightmares seeing all the lights shining. When the doodlebugs came over we would watch and pray they kept going over us. I can still see my mother's face now: she used to say if it passes over us before the engine stops we would be okay, then it would crash to the ground later.

My mother would take me fruit-picking out to Istead Rise. We would walk and it would take about half an hour. During one of these trips the siren went, and we ran into a little Sunday school until the all-clear sounded. The air-raids affected everything we did during the war. Although everything was frightening for everyone, we were all very happy and friendly.

Ration books limited the amount we had to eat. My mother would cook all day on Sundays, so we always had plenty of food. We didn't have many sweets. My father would mend our toys and I would take my doll to the Doll's Hospital to be repaired. Father mended our shoes with old bicycle tyres. We had chickens in the garden and we grew our own vegetables.

When the war was over, we would cycle over the farm fields to the Gravesend Aerodrome. In hindsight, it was the best time of our lives even though it was tough.

4

Anthony Galcius

I was serving mass in the Lithuanian Church when the war broke out. The suddenness and the wailing of the air-raid sirens took everyone by surprise. I looked over at my Mum in the front bench near the confessional. Panic stirred among the pews. The priest appealed for calm. He told the startled congregation that war had been declared at 11 a.m.

In fact, even before that Sunday, gas masks had been issued to all the population of the UK. Many London children had been evacuated. My mother would not let me out of her sight, so I did not join those thousands of children duly labelled with their names and destination. With the knowledge I have now of how some were treated, I am grateful to my mother for hanging on to me! My twenty-year-old brother Vince was conscripted into the Royal Army Medical Corps. My brother Joe, twenty-four, joined the Royal Artillery. Cazimir, twenty-two, was deemed unfit and never called up—strange, when of the three of them he probably was the fittest, playing football every Sunday on Hackney marshes! Later in the year, Anderson shelters were also provided for planting in the back yard. Constructed of six-foot-long corrugated steel sheets, which arched at the top, it was half in the earth and half above it, covered by the soil which had been displaced in the process. You climbed down into it via a small ladder, which was included in the package.

The first year of the war was often referred to as the 'Phoney War'. Sirens went off, everyone rushed to a shelter but then nothing happened. I knew quite a few friends who didn't even do that. They all just carried on as usual. We'd heard the grown-ups talk about fighting in France, bombings, ships sinking, and so on. I knew we were fighting the Germans, who were bad, really bad. This did not, of course, apply to the German Church in Adler St and Frau Simml. Somehow they were different.

Then one Saturday afternoon, 8 September 1940, I was walking down Buxton Street on my own, on the way back from St Anne's Church where I had been to confession. I was possibly thinking about my eighth birthday two and a half weeks previously, when my reverie was rudely interrupted by the warning siren wailing across the sunny blue skies. Another one of those false alarms, I thought. But then my mother's words came to mind: 'Whenever you're out and the siren goes, come home straightaway.' It took me three minutes to reach home, through the short cuts, past the back-to-back housing and cobbled streets, so characteristic of that area on the border of Bethnal Green and Whitechapel.

As I puffed through the front door, my sister Anne hurried me on, telling me that Mum was already in the Anderson shelter. My brother John was up the ladder leaning on the shed, wanting to see what was happening.

Although I'd asked my sister if she was coming down there with me, she'd opted to stay indoors. I did not fully appreciate that she couldn't have managed, anyway, to climb down into the shelter, because of her partially paralysed arm and leg.

As I went through the back door into the yard, I heard the drone of aircraft. I felt quite excited. Perhaps at last something was going to happen.

'Tony, hurry up and get down here,' my mother shouted, relieved that her youngest had arrived home safely. John, standing from his vantage point on the ladder, started to give us a running commentary. He pointed out the bombers flying in formation, like minute silver crosses.

Boom! Boom!

'That's the anti-aircraft guns,' John said excitedly. 'Tony, can you see tiny white puffs around the planes? They're the shells exploding.' I climbed down and stood in between the bunks. My Mum was lying on one of them.

Suddenly, John clattered off the ladder and dived into the shelter, as the first bombs began to fall. The guns intensified, the drone grew louder, and the bombs dropped nearer. Explosion after deafening explosion. Mum began sobbing.

'I want to die. I want to die,' she repeated.

She was to tell us later that the dreadful experiences of the First World War came rushing back at that precise moment. She had been so frightened, even though the few small bombs that fell on London between 1914 and 1918 were actually thrown out of the cockpit by the pilot of a bi-plane! She already had two babies to protect at that time, but at least her husband was alive to help. How was she going to cope now, a widow with a disabled daughter and an eight-year-old son, and all the worry about her four grown-up sons?

All this was too much for me. With Dad gone, what would I do if my Mum died as well, as she seemed to wish?

'Don't die, Mum, don't die,' I blurted out, crying like a baby, and clutching my mother's arms. We held each other, closed our eyes and prayed. Bombs exploded all over the docks, which were only about a mile away.

When we eventually emerged, after the all-clear had sounded, we could see huge fires in the direction of the docks. The pungent, acrid stink of smoke filled our nostrils.

Later that evening, the crimson red skies of the setting sun were mirrored to the east by the red glow of the still burning docks. Street and railway lights came on. So did the air-raid warning! The Luftwaffe was on their way back.

'We'll have to go to Bethnal Green Underground Station tonight,' my mother announced. 'At least down there we shall have a bit of peace.'

I was somewhat puzzled.

'Won't we have the noise of the trains if we go down the Tube, and where are we going to sleep?' I asked.

'No, Tony,' Mum answered, "there are no trains at the moment. They built the tunnels but hadn't had time to put the lines down when the war broke out. They've been made into shelters. So you won't hear any bombs, shells or guns.' Now, sixty years later, whenever I travel that section of the Underground from Mile End to Bethnal Green, I think of the trains running over where once my Mum and I slept in bunks.

'When will we go, then, Mum?'

'When the lights on the big lift go out, dear. It'll be your job to tell Mummy when they do, OK?'

The lift my mother was alluding to was part of a railway yard positioned right opposite our house. It was big enough to lift the goods trucks from ground level to the rail duct above adjoining the mainline. It was therefore a fair military target, despite being in the middle of a residential area. As enemy planes flew over the cliffs of Dover, warnings were telephoned to the lift operators long before the official siren sounded. All the lights were then turned off and the whole area plunged into darkness. If we left immediately we could get to the Tube shelter in five minutes.

The months that followed were to be the worst in my life as a child. They were probably also for the East End and the City of London. Day and night German bombers carried out intensive and extensive raids. Such was the regularity of day attacks that school was practically suspended. Classes were reduced to two hours a day from 10 a.m. until noon, which seemed to be the period least likely to have a raid!

Life took on a routine of its own. Every evening I would begin my vigil. My look-out posts varied from the upstairs front window to downstairs, or even just outside the front door. I would shout out, 'Mum, they're off,' referring to the lights on the railway lift, and she would gather her already prepared bundle of blankets and a bag containing essentials such as a flask of tea, toilet paper, sweets, and gas masks. Off we hurried to the Tube station.

The next day at 5.30 a.m., she would wake me as early as possible and tell me to go and wait for her in the park above while she folded the blankets and tidied up the bunks. We would then go home. Every day I would run on ahead to see if our house was still standing. Of course, it wasn't just the house we worried about, but about my sister and brother who slept in it during the raids. Once the parcel had been deposited, we would both then go to St Anne's, where I often served the 6 a.m. mass. Back home I'd be given breakfast and sent to bed for a couple of hours before going to school.

In the afternoon I would meet up with about five other kids on the street. If we weren't playing soccer or cricket, we would roam around assessing enemy damage. Fearlessly we would climb the rubble and search among the debris for the spoils of war! These consisted of shrapnel, bits of bombs, and parts of planes or its engines. Collections were begun and we were intensely proud of them. They were jealously guarded and only parted with after a fair deal of bartering. Some months later, much to my huge disappointment she threw out the whole collection that I had so carefully kept in a strawberry basket. It was a gesture of her wholehearted hatred of war.

After tea and a thorough wash as it got dark, I took up my vigil again, waiting for the lights to go off! Normally we heeded this 'secret' signal of ours immediately, but one evening we dithered. So we were still in the house when the warning sounded. We had not reached the top of our turning before we heard the sound of aircraft, like a giant's stentorian breathing in the sky. Bombs whistled down. As part of the psychological warfare, the Hun had fixed a contraption to the fin of the bomb which would cause a most terrifying screech, one only Hell itself could have created. I was terrified. My fear was exacerbated by the sight of my mother gripped by the same terror. I vividly recall her reaction that night. She screamed a prayer as she grabbed me and we both fell to the ground, her arms protectively around me. All I could do was shut my eyes tight and listen to the explosions as bomb after bomb dropped nearby. And this time they were much nearer. I was sure one had destroyed our house, just a few yards behind us. It had in fact landed two streets away. Still terribly close.

My Mum thought this was too close for comfort, and negotiated with another Lithuanian family to move into their bungalow in Chingford. The owner, Simeon Žalauskas, had known our family for many years. His daughter Mary was my sister Anne's best friend. Their family story had more than its fair share of tragedy. Mr Žalauskas was gassed three times during the First World War, having been forcibly conscripted into the British Army. He was given an ultimatum to join up or return to Lithuania. Mary's mother gave birth to three sons and a daughter and then spent twenty-one years in a 'home' suffering with depression. From a very early age, Mary had to take on the role of mother. Her eldest brother John died at the age of twenty-five, and her two other brothers were both born with hearing and sight difficulties.

But in 1940, Mary and her family gave my mother, sister, and me a very warm welcome, as we settled into their bungalow. Chingford was only up the road, but at least it was away from the East End, which had become such an intense target of German hostility. You could still hear the raids in the distance, though, and people were still frightened enough to want to seek shelter.

Shelter was found in a small park in Drysdale Avenue. A deep trench had been dug running parallel with the road. It was the length of a football pitch. The roof was a thick slab of concrete covered by soil. Along each side were twin bunks. Apart from toilets there were no other conveniences or luxuries.

For the few months we stayed in Chingford, I went to St Mary's School, adjacent to the Catholic Church of Our Lady of Grace and St Teresa of Avila. This meant a bus journey up King's Head Hill, quite long and steep, or a walk along the edge of the forest. Most of the time and after the initial two or three trips, when I was accompanied by my Mum, these journeys were done on my own or with other children.

About a mile away was a huge reservoir supplying water for North-East London. It was therefore a military target which was bombed occasionally and also defended by AA units of the Artillery. For a nine year old this meant shrapnel. The collection I had started at home continued here. I had my secret hiding place for it, which I shared with Mr Žalauskas. I recall his smiling comments about these items as he puffed away on his pipe, a smell which remains with me to this day.

As the Blitz on London began to diminish in the spring of '41, Mum decided it was time to return home.

5

Frances Clamp

Southend has been noted for its pier since the mid-nineteenth century. By 1889 it had been rebuilt as an iron structure, and the following year it acquired the first single-track electric tramway to operate in the country. In peace time it became an asset to the town but, as the Second World War loomed, it was a double edge sword, invaluable for unloading goods and the transfer of troops, but also a potential landing point for an invasion. Should it be partly destroyed or retained for military use? In the end the pier stayed and it was decided to evacuate as many school-aged children as possible.

In 1940 my six-year-old sister was to leave the town with other members of her school and it was decided that I, a mere three year old, should go with her. At that point our destination was unknown. I well remember going to Prittlewell Station with our mother, carrying my Mickey Mouse gas mask in a brown cardboard box and wearing a small haversack containing sandwiches on my back. I guess I must have had a case of clothes too, but that is something I no longer recall. What has stayed firmly in my memory is the smell of the steam train as it pulled into the station. To this day, visits to restored steam railways still remind me of then.

Being one of the youngest on the train, I was thoroughly spoilt by the older girls. We must have gone to London and then transferred to another station for our journey north, but again I have no memory of that experience. We eventually arrived in a mining town called Huthwaite, near the Nottinghamshire–Derbyshire border. With my sister Pamela I arrived at the home of Mr and Mrs 'B'. I always called them Aunty and Uncle 'B', although I guess the initial stood for a much longer name.

The B"s lived in a miners' terraced cottage in Common Road. Two other girls from the school were also billeted in the house and I shared a bedroom with my sister. As far as I was concerned this was an idyllic time. Years later I learned that the B's had lost a daughter who would have been my age. I think I became their missing child because I was loved and spoilt, an unusual happening for a middle child. (I also had a baby brother who had remained at home.)

Once a week a metal bath was placed before the fire and hair washing was unusual because a large jug was used to pour water over my head. Eyes remained tightly shut! With Pamela I went to Sunday school and also to a nursery school, which I loved. Our time in Common Road seemed to be one long, glorious summer.

After about six months my mother, grandmother, and brother also came to Huthwaite and took over part of a house called The Orchards. We left Common Road and I realise now that must have been a devastating time for our foster parents, although I remember little of the actual parting.

The Orchards was a large house rapidly falling into disrepair and only a few rooms could be used. I believe the owners had gone bankrupt some years earlier. Apparently the grounds extended for 3½ acres. There was a one-armed gardener, but much of the garden was semi-wild. A small stream ran through and I am told there was watercress growing. We weren't supposed to go far from the house, but on one occasion we did and met two soldiers in a remote corner of the garden. My mother was horrified to find us chatting away happily to them. This seems to have been my only real encounter with anyone to do with the war during our stay in Huthwaite.

Winter came. One morning we woke to find our mother paddling into our bedroom in Wellington boots. During the night the roof had leaked with disastrous results. On another occasion the washing froze on the line and my mother's dress stood up on its own in the kitchen before finally thawing out.

The kitchen sink was in front of a window and it was there that I used to have my bath. It was important to save water and I imagine less was used in an old-fashioned butlers' sink. On one winter's morning, as I sat in the sink, I remember looking out and seeing two cows peering back at me—an unusual and frightening experience for a townie! I expect they had broken down a fence to enter the garden.

My brother, Clive, had a large, all-enveloping, gas mask. As far as I know, this required pumping, a dangerous operation for a mother in the middle of an air-raid. We didn't have a shelter, but I don't remember ever hearing the siren during our stay. If there had been a raid, we would all have crouched under the dining room table.

By the spring of 1941 the fear of invasion via the pier had faded. The school returned to Southend and so did we. Our evacuation was over. I know many people have sad memories of this time but I can only say that, for me, it all seems to have been a great adventure, largely due to the helpful and friendly people who welcomed us to their village.

Paul Hopkins

Although I was born in 1940, I still have memories of the latter half of WW2.

At that stage we lived in Goring Road and I can remember my father being in the navy and seeing him walk up the road with his kitbag on his back. During this time, I would often at weekends go to stay with my grandparents. Sometimes I would be put on the bus (yes, alone) and sometimes my grandfather would pick me up in his old Austin 7. They lived on Cowdray Avenue, halfway to the fire station in Colchester. The No. 2 bus at that time would go from Parsons Heath, right round to North Station, as there was no Greenstead Estate built then. My mother would pay the conductor and ask for me to be let off at what was known as the by-pass stop. Grannie used to meet me then we would walk across the bypass to see my grandfather, who was an ARP warden. They had a hut on metal wheels on the north-west corner of the roundabout which was covered with concrete cones ready to be moved if enemy tanks should appear. I remember the other roundabouts were similarly adorned.

We used to sit in the old hut till his shift finished. I was given boiled water to drink; as there were no facilities laid on to the hut, I suppose they were frightened of contamination. I know the water tasted horrible. When he was on a night shift my grannie used to make me a cup of real cocoa before I went to bed and we would go round the house to check the blackouts were in place.

On nice days, I used to sit out on the grass verge watching the convoys go by. The Americans would throw me sweets and the occasional grapefruit. I particularly remember what was probably one of the last doodlebugs to go over. We were sat listening to 'Much Binding in the Marsh with Kenneth Horne' on the radio when my grandparents rushed out to see it with me behind, when the draught blew the door to, catching my toe underneath. At least I heard it with the motor running and we knew it wasn't going to land on us.

I can remember in the summer watching huge flights of bombers going over. At that time I didn't realise that there were airfields so close.

I have mentioned memories of my grandfather but my grandmother wasn't idle. She belonged to the WVS (Women's Voluntary Service). She would take me on to Colchester Station where they had a special canteen set up for the troops and along with a group of others she would serve the in-transit troops with tea and snacks while I sat on a stool behind the counter, just high enough to be able to see over the top. I remember there seemed to be hundreds of them coming and going. We used to call at the grocers and get something for Granddad's lunch when he was on duty, the aroma of coffee and bacon are still vivid today. In the grocers, there used to be a row of tins of biscuits all with glass lids, and I was allowed to help myself.

Every month in our street there were a group of people who used to arrange parties in an old tin hut. We had to have our own marked knife and spoon (we never had a fork). They would sit us children in rows. After the food, which consisted mainly of fish paste sandwiches and jelly (the jelly was separate) for 'afters', they would put on plays and sing songs for us. It doesn't seem much now, but it was a real treat then. I often used to wonder where they got all the food from.

For years after the war there were lots of the sheets of wire that had been used round the tables indoors which came in handy for making chicken runs. The older boys would use old aeroplane fuel tanks, apparently left behind for the scrap dealers to take from the airfield, to make into boats, and they would paddle on the River Colne. I suppose there was no point in shipping them back to the States. These things were about for a while after the war, even when I was ten and we moved. I suppose you could say that we benefitted from the war being in the country, which is what Colchester was then compared to London.

Funnily enough, I don't remember much about my father during the actual war except when he came home on leave. This was usually only a weekend in some cases and he used to bring us little things that he had made while on board. A child's perception of things was different then to what it is these days. The last thing I remember is the VE day party all the way up our street. It must have stretched over 100 metres. Heaven knows where they got all the tables.

Joy Blackmur

Well, I was only two years old when the war started, but I was 8 when it ended—so I remember the latter years as clear as day. Our small terraced house was in Maryland Point, Stratford E14 just up the road to our school, , Maryland Point School. Every day we would be given glass bottles of milk with a straw to drink and during the afternoon we'd lie down on little camp beds for half an hour's rest. Our teachers were strict and children were not allowed to speak unless spoken to. We all had to recite our times tables every morning and woe-betide those who did not know them. They got a slap round the legs and were made to stand in the corner.

During the war we three sisters all had a siren suit, an all-in-one with a hood. Mum always knitted us cardigans and pixie hoods, woolly hats which came to a point on top—we must have looked like garden gnomes! We'd wear a liberty bodice over our vests, which were like a waistcoat of cotton, with little rubber buttons down the front.

I can hear the 'Moaning Minnie' (the dreaded siren) even now, and Mum shouting, 'Never mind yer shoes—get down the shelter.' Seems a funny thing to say, but it was fun down the shelters, tucked up under the blankets surrounded by adults who always broke into song to keep our spirits up, as they handed round cups of tea. I always felt safe then. It was a way of life we just accepted as kids, we'd known no other. We took it as normal that Mum put up the blackout curtains at night and told us not to forget our gas masks as we got ready for school. The bomb sites were our playground and we went foraging for shrapnel with our tins and boxes.

The highlight of the week was when Mum dished out the sweet coupons. We were only allowed 3 oz a week. No wonder us war children were said to be the healthiest. I never had junk food and I remember lining up in school and given a spoonful of cod liver oil every day. Mum always gave us syrup of figs and a spoonful of Scott's emulsion every week. We were also given a chocolate button covered in Hundreds & Thousands, which were lovely till Mum told us they were worm cakes. She said, 'prevention is better than cure!'

There was a lot of heavy bombing where we lived in the East End. One night a doodlebug came over and Mum shouted, 'Quick—get under the table,' and I dived under with my two sisters. The whole house shook and part of the ceiling came down. We were lucky that night.

We were evacuated to Darwin, Lancashire for a year, and Mum came with us. We all wore wooden clogs there, even Mum.

At Christmas we all had a stocking with a doll (Mum made all the clothes for them) and a chocolate Father Christmas, a tangerine and a shiny penny in the toe, as well as a book each. Mum couldn't afford anything else. Even though Dad was away with the Army in India, Mum always made sure we had a happy time.

Glen Martin

I was born in Appledore in 1935, and so was ten years old when the war ended. One of my lasting memories as a child during the Second World War is first contact with non-Europeans, namely the American troops who were stationed here in North Devon, specifically to train for the D-Day Landings on the Normandy beaches.

There is an area on Torridgeside between Appledore (where I grew up) and Bideford where the landing craft were moored. I recall a long line of boats occupying the mud flats alongside a cause-way built to keep the tidal waters from flooding local farmland, owned incidentally by a farmer who would pay us sixpence a day when he needed help on his farm. We took full advantage of what was a natural play area for us among the farm buildings—when he wasn't looking, that is!

The American troops were a very friendly lot and it wasn't long before we were running around all over their craft. They knew about rationing and were very generous with cans of beans and chocolate. They seemed to have plenty of everything, especially chewing gum. I could never work out why gum was so popular with the Americans. I tried it and didn't like it at all. We were frequent visitors and enjoyed the friendly atmosphere there. One day we went for our free rations of canned food and chocolate only to find that all the moorings were empty—the Americans had left. Of course, they had moved out in preparation for D-Day, having completed their training on the beaches of North Devon. I have often wondered how many of them made it back to the States.

One of the most vivid memories I have is of two German airmen who were captured after crash-landing on Lundy Island in 1941. I would have been six years old at the time. Some years ago the navigator returned and his story was printed in the local paper. Rumour spread rapidly throughout the village (Appledore) that the airmen were to be landed at Appledore Quay, and crowds of very bloodthirsty Appledorians gathered at the slipway where they were due to be landed and handed over to the military. I was there, clutching Granddad's hand as usual. This was the first time in my life that I experienced collective hate, and I remember that I was frightened. A boat appeared with the captives and various armed military personnel. The authorities were quick to realise what would happen if they attempted to land the airmen there and the truck and soldiers waiting left hurriedly to pick the prisoners up farther up-stream, thus outwitting the would-be lynching party. (Appledore was a pretty rough place in those days.)

The barrage balloons were of interest to us kids, as were the huge billboards urging all to 'dig for victory' and to be aware that 'the walls have ears'. I recall the rationing, the Mickey Mouse gas masks that we had to take to school, and the drills we had to practise. The air-raid warden checking that no light escaped through the windows at night time. Also, we grew to recognise the engine sound of the German bombers as they occasionally flew over North Devon, presumably on their way to bomb Bristol and Avonmouth.

Lastly, I recall that we played a lot of football in the streets—with a tennis ball if we were lucky, but most of the time with an empty can (which didn't last long) and any piece of suitable wood which we could find (which did)! There was a craze for collecting cigarette cards (from empty packets found on the streets, or scrounged from adults). We seemed to spend a lot time running around the streets; I caught the bug, and am still doing it! We used to play hoops. This is done by buying a 'proper' iron hoop with an attached handle—not many had one of these, mostly the girls as I recall. We used discarded bike wheel rims, propelled in front of us while racing each other by whacking the bike wheel with a stick or a piece of wood. This involved a lot of running, so I loved it!

A final memory. Dad finally came home at the end of the war (we hadn't seen him for years) and my sister, then just five years old screamed and hid behind a chair as she didn't know who he was—he just walked in one day! He had been in the North African desert, then fighting in the Mediterranean, and then finally up through Italy, so he was burnt black by the sun. Welcome home Dad!

Vivian Sherry

I was born in 1942. One of my first real memories is standing on a dining room chair with a brown leatherette seat looking out of the living room window and calling to my Mum, 'the doctor is here.' I was about seventeen months old. He was visiting as I was recovering from diphtheria and within three weeks I caught scarlet fever. I was lucky to survive.

I can't recall trying on the gas masks, but I hate the smell of rubber—it makes me sick—and was later told babies were enclosed in their gas masks. This could have been the start of my fear of small places, which I have learned to control now.

My Dad drove a big lorry from Army depots to railheads and collected ammo and charges for bombs as war work. He was classed unfit for the forces, to my Mum's disgust, due to the effects of meningitis as a child leaving him quite deaf. Plus, he was also flat-footed.

Mum worked in various factories from the age of fourteen, ending up in one at Slough Trading Estate, sewing uniforms for the forces; stretching the Petersham stiffening to make the waist bands on the short jackets for the ranks. She said they were made an inch too small to save money. She was self-taught, but her dressmaking skills were legendary.

All clothing was on ration, as was food. We had a neighbour who, prior to the start of the war, had gathered up all sorts of stuff she thought might be hard to get; materials by the bale, all kinds, coating, shirting, dress weight; shoes, tins of fruit, canned goods, and so on. They were of Italian extraction and ran an ice-cream factory in Slough. I was good friends with their daughter Marianne. I remember eating with her under the dining room table, sitting on Mum's workbox side by side, with an oblong pie dish full of egg-custard made from dried egg and National Dried Milk, probably sweetened with saccharine, but with 'brown stuff' (nutmeg) sprinkled on top. There was a line drawn across the centre and we had a race to see who could eat up our half first. She always won.

We had few toys from older children in the family. Dad whittled items from wood for me, but paint was in short supply. What you have never had, you don't miss. He made me a box on wooden wheels, with two metal bars for axles, and a rope handle so I could take my rag doll for a ride up and down the garden path.

We were lucky, my parents had started to buy a small three-bed house opposite the Burnham railway line and the Slough Trading Estate just before the war started. We had an inside toilet and bathroom, too. There was a gas geyser over the top of the taps, and I hated the smell and the spiders! I remember being washed in the large china sink in the kitchen under the window, next to the stone-surrounded, copper boiler in the corner. Mum used to light a fire in the hole under the boiler with old bits of trees we picked up on our walk to the village; it got stuffed under the old Tansad pram on the chassis, and transported home. Fuel was rationed and hard to come by.

Our back garden was once lawn and flowerbeds, but 'Dig for Victory' changed all that! Dad dug it all over, creating small raised paths between rows of beds for vegetable growing. I remember 'helping' to weed out between the stuff growing so we would have food. When they dug up roots, maybe carrots or beetroot or parsnip, any worms I would feed through the fence to the chickens in the run next door. Once in a while we got two or three eggs back over the fence. What a treat—a real boiled egg, not scrambled egg made with powder which that slightly chemical taste. Mind you, if you had never eaten anything else much like me, it did not really matter. My Mum was good at using it for cakes and puddings; Dad reckoned her rice pudding was the best in the world.

We often had no lights and used oil lamps, if we had paraffin for them. If not, we used candles stuck onto saucers. The windows in my room were taped over with brown paper tape, to stop the glass from flying in if a bomb caused damage in the area. I had light-coloured curtains with black ones behind them so the light would not shine out at night.

At Christmas time, we had a real tree if Dad could find one on his trips; if not, Mum would pick a tree branch, not very big, and then it was painted with whitewash and stuck in a bucket with garden soil and stones. If we had any coloured paper the bucket was wrapped round and a length of bright material, a ribbon or even an old tie, was fastened round to keep the paper in place. Very cheery. Mum and I used to make bits to hang on the branches. She showed me how to make bobbles of wool to string up and hang. It must have been before I was three. We also collected milk bottle tops; some were cardboard disks with writing on, mostly red, and we used these after they were cleaned.

I don't remember getting a lot of presents; there was a stocking stuffed (it seemed to me) with a colouring book, a rag book, nuts, a small wooden toy my Dad had shaped, some stripy mitts my Mum had knitted from scraps of wool, and socks my Granny had made from unpicking one of her doilies she used to crochet before the war. I was happy enough.

I liked the company; we used to have the gramophone on and I was allowed to help Dad wind the handle to make it go. We had a cupboard full of records: The Ink Spots, Bing Crosby, and orchestral music, often from film scores. It was lovely. We would dance around wearing newspaper hats. We had home-made crackers with real things inside them, and we shouted 'Bang'. I got a small wooden spinning top, which I took a while to master. My Mum and Dad must have been working on the contents for ages. These things were precious, as all were hard to get.

My clever Mum was always sewing and knitting for me and other people. She taught me to knit by the time I was four. One of the best things I got was a lovely patchwork bedcover made from all the oddments left over from her work.

Granny used to do a lovely Sunday tea if anyone came, using her best cutlery. Little glass dishes were filled with jams and pickles and chutney and placed along the length. She made her own bread, when she could get the flour; only brown, to my Mum's disgust. Granny was well known for her lemon curd, which didn't keep well; in that house it didn't get a chance! No idea where she got the lemons. Another item was coconut macaroons, and they used the precious condensed milk which my Dad seemed able to acquire now and then. I am sure these things were not always there, but it's how I remember her house. A smell of baking and all the family crowded round the table. It was always warm there, too.

Granny had a closed fire in her kitchen. It had two brown enamel doors with little Bakelite windows so you could see the coals alight. This heated her water, but nobody had radiators run off it then. I liked her house, because she had a small area near the back door with a hatch to the yard. It was tin-lined, had a door on the outside, and the milkman used to leave her milk there. The mangle was in the space too, next to the wash boiler. I can remember standing on a stool and 'helping' her to 'dolly' the washing. (A dolly was a long handle with a bit on the bottom like a small four-legged stool. This acted like an agitator in a washing machine.) She would add a blue bag to the water, to keep the white items looking white. As the water cooled down, the items that could not be boiled were washed in the same water. When all was done, mangled and hung on the line, she would use the water, reheated on the stove in a metal bucket, to wash the kitchen floor. Nothing was wasted, soap was precious.

A short walk from our house was The Essoldo cinema. Mum was addicted to the Pathé News programmes. It was possible to get in without paying for a child under three, so she would scrape up a few pennies and go at least twice a week, to the matinée performance. The air-raids were quite frightening. We had one most nights, as we lived opposite the big trading estate. Bombers were not good shots and often missed the target. We were only one block away, and our house used to shake a lot. We were supposed to go down into the air-raid shelter we shared with the family next door. Mum hated the smells: no toilets, only a bucket, and there were spiders. After a few attempts, she decided the cupboard under the stairs was safe enough. Sometimes the bombers came early, with little warning. She would throw me under the bed mattress and lie on top, crying. The hairs on my arms still rise up when I hear the old air-raid siren in plays or on TV, even now.

At time like these and, indeed, for many years to come, visitors never came empty-handed. A few tomatoes, an onion or two, odd bits we did not grow; all was welcome. Mum made beetroot and onion chutney, tomato jam, and green tomato chutney. Fruit was mostly bottled for the winter time.

Gran had bowls in her kitchen for the fat dripping; one for beef, one for pork, and one for lamb. Gran would turn the chosen bowl upside down to get the jelly for a slice of stale toasted bread, after the mould was trimmed off. I got the job of toasting it on a long handled fork, by the open fire. Dripping was horrible, it made me sick to eat, so I didn't get it twice. The fat was used like butter on the toast, with the jelly added on like jam. Yuk!

I ate a lot of raw berries and vegetables from the garden, bread with a smear of jam, eggs (sometimes powdered), and stews. Mum's was mainly root vegetable and bones. My Dad tried to get me to drink hot milk—how I hated it. I was years older before I discovered I didn't mind it chilled. When I was about eight, a young doctor back from the wars told my Mum how my stomach could not digest dairy foods and fats in particular. So all the rich cream, milk, cheese, and butter she was stuffing me with after it became more readily available was not doing me any good at all. No more cod liver oil, hooray!!! I could have honey, sweets, jam; no toffees or chocolate. As it was all on ration, I did not get much.

The first Christmas after the war was finally over was amazing. Rationing eased a little, and Mum scrounged enough stuff to make a reasonable Christmas cake. The best bit for me was waking up that morning and seeing Santa had really been. My stocking was stuffed with the usual sort of thing. I didn't understand why my Mum was so insistent on me going downstairs. It was cold, as usual, and bed was warmer. She grabbed me, put on my old dressing gown (a cut down coat) and socks, I opened the room into the living room and was shocked. It seemed to me the whole room was full of toys, like a picture in one of my old books of a shop window. I crept in and just looked. I found out later, the entire family and some of our friends had raided all the shops to give me a treat. Toys had started to slowly come back into the shops. There was a real doll, with hair. My Granny had knitted clothes for her, including a coat and hat and boots. A skipping rope with wooden handles painted in red and blue stripes; a wonderful pair of scales, with two little silver metal pans to balance on a beam, some real tiny sugar sweets to weigh, and a new book to read in bed. My Mum insisted I went to the kitchen to eat. Leaning against the side of the cooker was a dark red bike, with just two wheels. I was bowled over. Until then, I had always ridden a trike like a maniac. I was stunned into silence. My Dad took me out to try the new bike which was far too big for me. I was allowed to play with the toys in the front room, while Dad was instructed to come up with some wood blocks to add to the pedals so I could ride it. (Mum had put my name on the list at the bike shop two years before, so I got a much desired bike.) It took me until the spring to get the hang of balancing it. Then I did circles in the road, managing to take the skin of my toes, which were hanging out of my sandals which had the toes cut out. Shoes were not easy to find and required coupons. I was threatened with losing the bike, and suffered a week with it locked in the shed.

Shirley Snell

I was two and my sister Hazel six when war broke out. We lived in Ipswich and were evacuated to Leicester. Because I was young, my mother came with me to one house and Hazel lived further up the road with a very nice family in another house. We had our gas masks with us and mine was shaped like a Donald Duck face. My Dad was a soldier in the war and was stationed in North Africa.

After some time we went back to our home in Ipswich. As we lived near to an American Airbase, we had one of the airman's wives called Kitty stay with us. One of our favourite sayings at that time was 'got any gum, chum?' I learned to say this at a very young age. We had air-raid shelters in our road, just outside our row of terraced houses, but my mother preferred us to go into the cupboard under the stairs as soon as the air-raid warning siren sounded. A warden used to come round to see if we were okay, and as soon as the all-clear siren sounded we came out of the cupboard and got on with our lives. We were happy.

As soon as I turned five I went to St Helen's School with my sister, but then when she was eleven she went to the big school (as we called it), Christchurch Central. We had air-raid shelters in our playground and I remember that, after the war, at playtime we used to play in them after being told not to. One day we were summoned to the headmaster's room, where we got the cane. I remember us waiting outside his room rubbing soap on our palms, so it would slip and not hurt so much.

We had happier times when Dad finally came home from the war. I recall he brought home with him an 18-inch-long stick which was all chiselled out and burnt with dates and country names. He said they had done this to keep them occupied. We called it 'Daddy's little gun'. To this day we still use it as a towel rail in one of our bedrooms.

Nigel John Austin

I was born in 1930 in Chapel House, Thorpe-Le-Soken, Essex. My earliest recollections are of my father making black out shutters for his shop and our home. The latter were made of a wooden frame made of splines covered with cardboard and wire netting with old cycle inner tubes used to form seals round the edges.

My Uncle Peter joined the Royal Corps of Signals before the war as a driver, because he expected the war to come and wanted to select which part of the Army himself. He was sent to France, evacuated via Dunkirk wearing only a pair of ladies' pants. His younger brother was eventually called up into the Royal Artillery. He manned a new anti-aircraft rocket battery and was sent to the USA to demonstrate it there. He had the opposite experience to Peter, touring the country, and had a whale of a time; he visited Hollywood and Mexico and saw no action at all.

Very early in the war we were issued with gas masks, rather rubbery and claustrophobic. When war broke out I was attending a small private primary school in the next village. When I was eleven I attended the High School for Boys in Colchester. I would cycle the ¾ mile to the station, catch a train to Colchester North then a bus into town, and continue the rest of the journey on foot. Some of the carriages were really old, with gas lighting. As there was a shortage of teachers they would have to double up on subjects. The gym master took dictation; the Maths, English composition, and English master, Geometry, as he had been a draughtsman at Paxmans Engineering Works.

As sweets and bread were rationed, we bought Horlicks tablets and OXO cubes to lick. A bread coupon entitled one to buy four buns which could be sold individually for 100-per-cent profit.

Nearly all windows had tape stuck to the glass. Those in towns could have air-raid shelters. My uncle and aunt had an Anderson shelter in their back garden and grew vegetables on top of it. He was a railway engine driver so did not have to join up. My school shelter was dug at the end of the headmaster's garden where we had to go whenever there was an air-raid. I remember that we sang popular songs when we were down there, like 'You are my Sunshine' and 'Roll out the barrel'. My clothes consisted of three sets of school uniform: one for 'best', to wear to places like Church; the second for school; and the oldest to play in. It was the accepted thing to make do and mend. Walking and cycling were the norm for us.

My father had damaged lungs due to TB so was not called up. We accepted an evacuee from East London, a boy called Frank. He experienced a real culture shock, returning to London in time for the Blitz.

The coast was out of bounds with barbed wire entanglements, mines, and pillboxes. We were fortunate in Thorpe, in that we had access to seawater at Landermere-on-Handford Water, which was a tidal backwater. Roundabout there were searchlights and ack-ack batteries, which were frequently moved about so that the enemy wouldn't know where to expect them. A tank trap was dug from the backwaters to past Weeley, deepening Holland brook in parts. Pillboxes were built in many places and tank obstructions in Thorpe high street at its narrowest part with concrete cones and railway sleepers which fitted into holes in the road if required. A battery of 25-pounders was installed in Station Road and one of the howitzers at Landermere. Soldiers were quartered in the large empty houses and some in Nissan huts. Many houses in Clacton and Frinton were unoccupied, becoming ghost towns.

Living in the country, we lived better than most. People caught wild rabbits, reared chickens and pigs, and grew vegetables and fruit. Every piece of land, however poor, was cultivated. Coal became in short supply and I can remember my father breaking up old radio cabinets for firewood. Only a few motor vehicles were allowed to be used. They had a label fitted to the inside of the windscreen with 'CD IV EL' on it. The headlights were masked with just slits to restrict the light. Petrol was rationed. The Eastern National bus went over to gas produced by burning wood chips in a large cylinder towed behind it with a large flexible tube to the engine. The power was poor. Passengers having to get out and walk up hills and could be up to two hours late.

As boys our most popular pastime was playing soldiers and having mock battles. We did have toy tin hats. Our transport were hambones (go-carts), constructed out of a wooden box fixed to one end of a plant with a set of pram wheels beneath. The front end of the plank was bored with a red-hot poker heated in one of our mums' kitchen fires. A cross piece of wood was also bored and bolted loosely to the plank at right angles with another pair of pram wheels. Ropes were fixed to the cross piece so that it could be steered.

I was a Boy Scout, and one of our activities was to act as German paratroops in Weeley and the Home Guard were to intercept us. The first time we won, but not the second. The Home Guard was a real 'Dad's Army'. One member was of a nervous disposition. When on the firing range, his first bullet went high over the butts, the second hitting the ground a yard in front. He was not allowed to shoot anymore. The Home Guard was composed mainly of those in reserved occupations; my wife's father was in the Home Guard and sometimes had to do sentry duty at Stone Point in Walton. His rifle was kept in a corner at his home.

The nearest bomb was an incendiary dropping about 40 yards behind our house near the Baptist chapel, hitting the curb, bouncing off, just missing the wooden chapel by no more than 2 feet, and setting a wooden fence and hedge alight. Luckily it was extinguished by the ARP wardens. It was quite exciting visiting bomb craters and crashed planes, collecting pieces of the Perspex windscreens to make finger rings. We also collected spent and live ammunition. Once I came home with three live .303 bullets; my mother was so cross she threw them into the lighted copper furnace—luckily when they exploded no real damage was done, they only blew open the furnace door. My mother was so shocked she stopped scolding me. The V1s had a distinctive engine sound and we used to wait for it to stop. After about a minute they had glided to the ground and then exploded unless they were hit by ack-ack fire, then it could fall too close for comfort. The V2 rockets came unannounced. There were two loud bangs, one when it came through the sound barrier and the other when it exploded. The nearest one to us was about 1½ miles away beside a road and making a huge crater about 40 feet wide and 30 feet deep, demolishing a pair of unoccupied houses opposite.

Marian Thornton

I was seven years old when the war started. My parents ran a grocery store in Exeter. I remember my father took my brothers and me to the seaside. The beach was covered in scaffolding, no doubt to hinder the enemy should they try to invade.

This must have been my Dad's way of saying goodbye to us because he joined the Army and we didn't see him for years, as he was sent to Ceylon, India, and Burma.

Back in England, we had to survive the bombing of Exeter. The Blitz I remember well. A siren went off during the night and as we didn't have a shelter, we huddled together under the dining room table, listening to the explosions, always wondering whether the next one would land on our house. When the bombing had ceased, I went outside and looked towards the city—it was ablaze.

My grandparents had a farm a few miles outside of Exeter. I would cycle to see them when I could. Sometimes my brothers would come along and we would cross the stream and play in the field behind the farmhouse. One day I strayed a little and found something sticking out of the ground. It was the tail of an incendiary bomb.

Food was very scarce and it was usual to see people queuing for ages for any sort available besides the usual rationing. I helped my mother serve in the shop and I would deliver goods while my brothers were allowed out to play.

All the doors and windows at my school were blacked out to prevent shattered glass in the event of being bombed. This meant that if the teacher was out of the class you could not see when she was returning. One day the teacher had to attend a meeting and we were left for some time without her. The rest of the class wanted to know if she had the test papers in her desk. Like a fool I volunteered to look. I was in the middle of searching her desk when all of a sudden the door opened and in she came, wanting to know what I was doing. 'I am tidying it for you, Miss!' I said. 'Go and sit down,' was her reply.

I must have been about ten when my mother sold the business and we moved into a house with an extra bedroom (because up to then, four children shared the same room and beds). In the dining area a metal cage shelter was already installed—more protection than a table.

Although we had an extra bedroom and front room, as it was known then, we didn't have a bathroom. We used to keep a long bath hanging on the all outside and on bath nights we had a system of queuing up for a bath using the same water. This was because the water had to be heated on the top of the gas stove. Children really do not know how lucky they are today. The toilet was situated outside.

We lived opposite the County Ground and I remember seeing the ground covered in tents. The American soldiers were living there at the time. One day they were there the next day they had disappeared off to D-Day, although we didn't know this at the time.

Money was very short too in those days and when my eldest brother got himself a paper round I thought what a good idea. We never had pocket money. Paper girls were not heard of in those days but that did not put me off. I was taken on and delivered papers every morning before school, plus Saturdays and Sundays. Some mornings we would all have to wait in the shop for delivery of the papers because of the bombing in London during the previous night. Trains were late and because of this, extra pressure was put on the owner of the business. Her husband was an Army officer serving in France. I knew I had to get to school on time so decided to help my boss by preparing my own paper round for delivery, as I knew exactly who had what and on which days of the week.

I used to run all the way to school at times because the hem of my blue coat had been let down and as the coat had faced, the hem was darker than the rest of the coat. I hated it, but both money and clothing coupons were scarce.

At the age of fourteen I had to leave school. I tried to stay on, but because of the timing of the changeover from fourteen to fifteen my request was turned down. I do remember that during the last year I was in the top class of the school and hovered in first, second, and third places in exams. I have always regretted having to leave school at such an early age, just when I seemed to be doing so well.

My mother steered me into an apprenticeship with a high-class tailoring business where I worked for about a year. My newspaper boss had other ideas for me. She persuaded and paid for me to take a commercial course at a local private college. My mother was not happy about this, and after the first course said that I had to pay for the lessons myself out of my earnings from the tailoring job. My wages were 15s a week at the time.

I have never regretted taking the commercial course because, when competent after a year, I managed to secure an office job and climbed the ladder little by little until I landed a senior position both at home and abroad.

I am now eighty years old and after all this time, I can still recollect the sound of our planes roaring overhead at night, hour after hour it seemed.

13

Michael C. Goodey

I was born in Halstead, Essex, on 20 September 1938. This area being a non-specific target, the day-to-day events of the war had little effect on us as children. Some do stick in my mind, however. One of these was the regular air-raid practise at school, when we all had to leave the classroom and go into the shelter in the playground—a damp, dark place that regularly flooded in wet weather—and sit on wooden benches. If the shelter was flooded, we all had to hide under our desks instead.

I also remember the huge excitement when we were all called outside at home to watch a lone doodlebug fly over. It was one that had obviously lost its way, but for us it was exciting. Of course we had no knowledge that what was excitement for us, was injury or death for someone else.

Although Halstead was untouched, we were only 15 miles from Colchester. Here was a very large military base and an important port, so planes would fly over to bomb it, especially at night. When this happened the air-raid sirens would go off and we were either hustled under the stairs or taken out into the Anderson shelter which Dad had built in the garden.

We lived quite close to some hostels for Land Army girls, and of course this used to attract the Americans. We would wait and try the 'any gum, chum?' and more often than not it would succeed. It was pure heaven to have a stick of chewing gum.

We came from a rather poor area, so the shortages of food during and after the war made little difference to us. Dad had an allotment and a large garden so we had plenty of vegetables. We also kept rabbits and we never wondered why some kept disappearing after we had rabbit pie. Chickens kept us supplied with eggs. I do know that the first banana I had I ate it, skin and all. I didn't know you had to peel it first.

Clothing was a different matter, being on ration, and I was always dressed in my elder brother's clothes, cut down to fit; more often than not, if I had a hole in my shoes, Mum used to put a piece of cardboard in. This was sufficient when it was dry, but if it rained that was a different matter.

When we had to go under the stairs during an air-raid, we had to put our gas masks on. Mine was a Mickey Mouse one. I wonder how many youngsters would do that today. While it would seem a little naïve to say it, we knew little about the war. Even at the age of seven, remember that we were not as sophisticated as young people are today.

My Dad was an air-raid warden. He would go out after we were in bed. Neither of our parents ever spoke about it or talked to us about anything. We were happy with what we had. There was no competition as to who had the best designer shoes or clothes.

Perhaps it was best that we didn't know what was going on. Maybe our parents thought that there was no point in worrying children unnecessarily. I do know that we went about our lives in complete ignorance of the death and destruction going on elsewhere, and perhaps 'ignorance is bliss' after all.

14

John Cannell

Born in 1938, my earliest recollections are of course of the war with Germany. I didn't understand the horror of it all then and it was all like a big game. Even playing on bomb sites that had been inhabited houses days before was just great fun! The sweet innocence of youth!

The bombs did not frighten me either, at least not enough for me to remember it now. Apparently I didn't like the 'wind' after they exploded, but I had no concept of death. Seeing the V1 flying bomb was a real treat, though I only remember a few. It was essentially a 1,800-pound bomb fitted with stubby wings and an impulse duct engine. The engine did not have a propeller but worked by taking in air and fuel which then exploded, forcing shutters at the front to close, hence projecting the exhaust gases out the back. This happened forty or forty-five times a second, thus making a distinctive buzzing noise which resulted in one of its nick-names, the 'Buzzbomb'. A little wind vane at the front gave a very approximate measurement of distance travelled and when it was theoretically over the target, the engine cut out and the controls pushed the machine into its final dive—but this was so inaccurate that it could not even be sure of hitting a city the size of London. It was quite fast, between 350 and 400 mph, so that only our latest fighters could catch it. However, it could only fly in a straight line and at a fairly low altitude so the radar-guided anti-aircraft guns were very successful.

The sight of those stubby wings, the long engine above the rear fuselage, and the buzzing noise they made are still clear in my mind. I remember distinctly a time when Derek (my twin brother) and I were with our mother and a neighbour, Mrs Joslin, and her son Peter. We were walking in Wanstead Park when we heard and saw a V1 flying towards us. We all jumped in a ditch, but Derek and I had our heads up watching it. Peter, who was a year younger than us, asked what would happen if it dropped on us. 'It will blow our heads off,' we shouted, roaring with laughter as Peter started crying.

Sometimes we used to go to a shelter at the bottom of our garden during an air-raid, sometimes just down the cellar under the house. We preferred the cellar because it wasn't as cold and damp as the shelter, not realising that, with its thick concrete walls and half buried in the ground, the shelter was much safer.

A brother, Graham, was born on 4 April 1944. We had not intended to join the evacuation, but Graham had whooping cough and the doctor said he could not guarantee him surviving the damp conditions in the cellar or the air-raid shelter. Shortly afterwards, we (including our mother) were evacuated to a place called Wroxham, near Norwich. We were picked out as being the most respectable looking family out of a pretty bad bunch, and were taken to stay with a Lady Hastings in what seemed to me to be an enormous mansion named Bureside. We were housed in an attic and mixed mostly with the servants. Graham slept in a drawer! We had a good time there, but one episode stands out more than any other. That was an adventure that must have caused people a lot of worry.

The gardener kept a lovely vegetable garden, with rows of neat plants including what I now know were onions gone to seed. Derek and I were chasing each other about this garden when suddenly I was horrified to see that we had broken one of these plants, and even more horrified to find that the gardener had seen us do it! He yelled at us and we ran for our lives. I ran up to the attic and hid under the bed.

I remember someone coming in to look for me and as they looked under the bed I wriggled round and hid behind the chair. When they went to look behind the chair I wriggled back under the bed. Having searched the house they then went to look outside.

There was a river (the River Bure) running across the bottom of the garden and I found out afterwards that they thought I might have drowned in it. The police, local search-light crews, and all sorts of other people were out looking, and my fear and determination to stay out of sight increased when looking out of the window I saw Derek being taken away by the local policeman. I assumed to prison; actually, of course, just to help in the search. I don't remember how I was found, but I do remember being a bit embarrassed at all the fuss and being made to apologise to various people.

Other memories include my introduction to Rupert the Bear during school story time, visits to Mundesley for a rare look at the sea and sand, and a taste of still warm goat's milk which I thought was revolting.

We went back to London later, in time for the V2 rockets, though not being able to see them meant that they made little impression on me. The V2 was the world's first long-range ballistic missile, comprising a warhead of about 2,000 pounds on top of a rocket motor and guidance system. They were about as inaccurate as the V1, but caused quite a bit of damage if they did land in an occupied area. The frightening thing was that because they flew several times faster than the speed of sound, there was no warning of their arrival and no chance of intercepting them.

For a child of the age I was then, the war was just a bit of an inconvenience. I had no idea of the real effect on the country or the misery caused to countless families. Still less did I think about the fact that, during the later stages of the war, the Germans were suffering far more than we ever did, with whole cities pounded into rubble by our heavy bombers, and people roasted or suffocated in their shelters by the fire storms that swept through some of the more combustible towns. Even if I had thought about what was happening to the Germans, I wouldn't have worried. We were taught (the population at large, by the newspapers and radio that is, not in my case by my parents) that the Germans were all evil. Whatever happened to them, they deserved it. It was only later that I gradually realised that this was rubbish. The people who had started the war were not the men in the street; as with all wars, it was the dictators and politicians.

15

Mrs Dorothy Waller

When the war started I was three years old and our family was living at The Cottage, Weeley Heath. My father worked on College Farm, Weeley. This was situated between Weeley Heath and Great Bentley and just 6 miles from the coast at Clacton-on-Sea.

As a farmer, my father didn't serve in the frontline of the war but was instead in the Home Guard, which required practising with guns in preparation to 'guard the coast'.

At the age of five in 1940, I attended Weeley School. The most poignant reminders of everyday school life were the sound of doodlebugs, the air-raid siren, and the air-raid shelters that we had to escape to. There was a brick shelter in the playground where the teachers escorted us when we heard the familiar wail. It had a doorway 'in' and at the opposite end the 'out' route was a hole, low down. To get out we had to crawl on our hands and knees. All I remember is the cold and dampness as we sat huddled together while we waited out the bombs. When the number of children grew, there was not enough room for us all in the shelter so the elder children had to walk down the road and take refuge in the semi-circular arches under the railway bridge.

However, the most frightening times were when the air-raid siren would sound as we were on the way home from school. It was either while walking the narrow roads between the fields or at night, when my younger sister and I would put on our 'siren suits' (all-in-one garments) and hide in the cupboard under the stairs with my parents. As doodlebugs (flying bombs) passed over, we would just pray that they wouldn't fall on us when the noise stopped. It was also common in those days for incendiary bombs to be dropped all around the house and once we heard the crunch of a bomb landing on the roof. Luckily it didn't explode.

Another thing that sticks in my mind is that we had to carry a gas mask with us at all times. Although quite an ominous bit of equipment, it became part of our daily routine. The other thing I will never forget is the darkness. Lights were not allowed due to the 'blackout' so night-times were always so dark, especially since woods surrounded our cottage, namely Maldon Wood and Tofts Wood. My father made shutters to put over the windows so that we could use paraffin lamps inside. We would often see searchlights and barrage balloons in the sky in the direction of Harwich.

American soldiers were stationed in the woods near our cottage. I remember one day being frightened as I walked down the lane and saw the camouflaged faces of soldiers hiding in the trees and just a few metres away. It was an eerie time as there was so much activity at night that you could hear but not see.

I also recall the food. Living on a farm we were lucky to be able to eat from the garden. Although there were no oranges, banana, sweets, crisps or the variety of foods that people don't give a second thought to today. We also had ration books, clothing allowance books and identity cards.

The supply of everything was controlled. There was no electricity. We used candles and oil lamps and cooked on an oil stove. The radio we had ran on accumulator batteries which were changed every two weeks by a delivery man. We collected water from a well in the garden and the toilet was a bucket with a wooden seat over the top. Cut up newspaper served as toilet paper.

When we needed to travel into town, usually from Weeley to Maldon, we would take a bus with no lights, powered by a generator that was pulled behind. There were hardly any cars, only bikes. Barbed wire lined the beaches and many shops were boarded up. Iron gates and railings were taken away to be melted down and used to manufacture items and weaponry for the war. All the signposts had been removed so they would not assist the enemy.

In 1946 we moved to College Farm which belonged to my grandparents. German prisoners would work on the farm. They were friendly and made toys and autograph books for us. My mother would make tea and sandwiches which I would take to them in the barn.

One day, as my father was ploughing the field with a tractor, the sound of a fighter plane was heard, which grew closer and closer finally coming down in the field. My father brought the American pilot home for tea before a jeep from a nearby airbase arrived to collect him. His name was 1st Lt C. E. Wheat Jr, USAAF. Several years after the war, he wrote to my father, Mr Lance Lord, to thank us.

On another occasion, a plane crashed into the trees at the side of the field at night. My father went out to investigate and came home with a grim face. He had found the pilot dead near the wreckage.

In 1945, my sister and I went to stay at my aunt's newspaper shop in Maldon High Street. We were there when the war ended. To celebrate, there was a large bonfire in the street.

Thomas Stock

Born in Plaistow, East London, I was exactly five years and two months old when war was declared. Prior to the war, my only memories were of starting school, going to Sunday school (which I loved), and my grandfather's fruit and vegetable shop. His shop was situated on the corner of the street opposite the big school I attended. I loved my visits to Spitalfields Market with my grandfather as he picked up the goods in his pony and cart. Then came the blur of the Blitz. The school playground was taken over by a massive shelter, huge silver-grey barrage balloons hung in the air, and searchlights beamed in the night skies. Noise, bombs, and more bombs!

On one memorable glorious sunny day I was sitting up in a tin bath outside the kitchen window, when the wail of the air-raid siren started, closely followed by aircraft and bombing. I was suddenly grabbed out of the bath, wrapped in a towel and rushed down the garden to the shelter. The same shelter, that was a few months later, to save mine and my families lives when bombs landed behind my grandfather's shop four or five doors away. It once came too close and my parents were forced to move home. My vivid memory is of being carried to safety on the shoulders of an ARP warden.

Briefly we moved to Bedford, where I attended school for a time. Here we shared a house, which was a common experience in those times. This was to be very short-lived, as we moved back to Stratford to a flat above an undertaker's shop. The glass-sided hearse and lovely black horses became a familiar sight. This was to be the end of city life for us, as my father had joined the Army on the eve of our evacuation to the North Essex countryside.

Here we shared a house with a mother and daughter in Little Yeldham. It was here that we later moved into a home of our own. These were houses built to house families suffering from the depression in the North-East of England with a large garden area and an opportunity to create a new life for themselves.

This, however, was not the end of the war for me. Just three fields away from the back of our house was just one of the hundreds of air bases built for our defence and then attack and return the war to Germany. By the time I was ten years old, I had a full bandolier of .303 bullets and a burned-out flare pistol taken from an aircraft that had crashed near to the vicarage. An American airman had given me a guided tour inside a super fortress from the cockpit to the tail gunner and I had siphoned petrol from the wing tank of a crashed mustang fighter plane.

Anne Chisholm

My sister and I were evacuated from Forest Gate, East London. We were instructed to go to school as normal with a sandwich for lunch; this went on for several days until we were mustered and taken to a railway station. My mother made me promise not to be parted from my younger sister, and she had no idea where we were going.

It was a long journey as we constantly stopped in tunnels I believe to avoid being strafed by German planes (hearsay), and needless to say we had eaten our sandwich as soon as the train pulled out from London. Eventually we arrived in St Austell in Cornwall, a place I had never heard of. There were tables of food laid out by the WI which were very welcome.

We were then lined up to be picked by prospective carers. As we were a pair we were not popular. Eventually we were 'allocated' to a thin, miserable looking woman and taken to a village known as Fraddon. The end terrace cottage was immaculate and her husband cheery (he was a miner in the clay pits). They had no children of their own. We were not popular with the local children, who called us 'vacees'. Our house had no water, no electricity, and no indoor sanitation, which was some way down a communal garden where we often encountered rats.

My sister, a biddable little girl, settled in. Our lunch was an OXO cube with water and a slice of bread. I had taken a scholarship prior to evacuation and was offered a place in either Newquay or St Austell. Obviously, they could have been in France for all I knew. I chose Newquay. Mrs Cole, my carer, was proud. She was always 'Mrs Cole'. I can now appreciate how she disliked having us around. No children of her own, and to keep face in the village she agreed to take one evacuee and then got landed with two. My father came to visit us while on embarkation leave and my sister and I agreed to say we were happy so as not to let him take any worry to war. He was sent to Singapore.

One day, my sister and I were sent to collect a battery for the radio; she slipped and the acid went on her knee. It wouldn't heal and my mother was sent for. She then took her home, which was now in Southend. Of course, as a mother she quickly sussed out the situation and I was immediately re-billeted to a very nice couple. I then went home for a holiday and did not return, spending the rest of the war in Southend.

On my return to Southend there were no schools open at the time, and my mother sent me to a small private school, but as my father was missing presumed killed she only had a widow's pension plus what she earned as a nurse. So, I was removed and went on a part-time secretarial course (bang went my dreams of going to university). When she could longer afford this, I worked in the afternoons for the school to pay my tuition fees. When I heard my father was a POW, I thought I was lucky he wasn't killed like the fathers of many of my peers. I was relieved, as then I had no idea of the atrocities the Japanese committed in the camps. In the meantime my mother had found someone else believing my father dead, so there was much difficulty when he eventually returned. He bought presents for my sisters and me as he still thought of us as children. He showed us photos he had kept of us taken at the beginning of the war, it was now six years later. I can remember him sobbing in his bed at night, and there was no comforting him.

The war was still in full swing in Southend, with the planes from Germany carrying out raids. One day on my way home I was forbidden to go down the road I lived in, as a bomb had been dropped on the corner. This may surprise you but I found this part of the way we lived. My mother used to sit with us under the Morrison table telling us to keep our bums in. Eventually we stayed in bed, and Mum came in the room with us so that if a bomb hit the house we would all go together. After the bombing came the doodlebugs, and when the engine stopped any person in the street dropped to the ground without thinking.

Our life was hard and food was short. Many a time my mother would say she wasn't hungry and go without. It did not occur to my sisters and I that there just was not enough to go around.

The Americans came with their sweets and ice-cream to give us, but we thought it was a waste and they should have bought guns and bombs. At this time I had lived through a war and could not see any end. Then one day the lights came on—in just one shop, granted, but it was amazing. My sisters and I did not celebrate VE day, as at that time our father was still a prisoner of the Japanese.

Life was hard but we put up with it. This has served me the remainder of my life, and for my generation nothing has been bad for such a long period. I am grateful for the time I have had since so many lost their lives and their health.

18

Isabelle Alexander

I was fourteen when war broke out in 1939. I lived in Forres, a small town about 25 miles east of Inverness, Scotland, with my parents and older sister, Elsie. Our house, Firthview, was large and my mother took in lodgers. I turned fourteen on February 26th and left school at Easter. I went to work in the local newsagents, Watsons, delivering the newspapers on a high bike with a basket in the front and progressed to working behind the counter. When war was declared my parents were on holiday in Blackpool (a help came and kept an eye on us and the lodgers) and they bought us gold signet rings with the date '3.9.39' engraved inside and our initials on the front. I still wear mine.

I remember gas masks being issued, and how they had a horrible rubbery smell. No one carried them around and we never once wore them. Forres was such a small town; we felt protected and unaffected by the war. Perhaps this was just a typical teenage sense of immortality! I remember a siren going off only once. We had a cellar in our house which we retreated to, but my father stayed outside looking up into the sky and nothing happened!

We were not affected by rationing either. We kept chickens and grew vegetables. There were local farms and I never remember food being unavailable. One or two of our lodgers worked for the farmers and brought food back with them. My father also kept pigeons which were used by the Army for carrying messages. They would come and collect them by motorbike and after their 'war work' was complete they would fly back home.

When I was fifteen I went to work at Gordons, a costumier. I helped with alterations and went to 'posh' houses to help dress the ladies in the clothes they had ordered. I earned 7s 6d a week. One particular memory I have is how I helped Mr Gordon tie up parcels of knitted socks and Cadbury's chocolate for his two sons, Wilfred (a chemist) and Harold (an artist) who were POWs in Germany. This method has stayed with me; I still tie up presents with fancy ribbon and never use cello tape. I didn't have fancy clothes. They were simple dresses bought from a little shop in town and when I worked at the newsagents I would wear an overall.

I recall a farm in Kinloss had been taken over by the RAF, rented by the Air Ministry. Kinloss is 3 miles from Forres. The townspeople were pleased because it meant jobs at the air base for the men who weren't fighting. There was a cinema and transport was provided to the base. The youngsters used to count the bombers coming in and out, and got to know all the planes. They flew very low. I suppose there were dangers, having the base so nearby but it was never bombed. I think it was too far up North and not within the range.

As time went on my mother was given the choice of taking in three Glasgow evacuees or three airmen from Kinloss. She chose the latter, and these were an Egyptian, a Cockney, and a Scotsman. Mother earned 6d a night and only had to give them a bed, although I'm sure she gave them food too.

When I was sixteen I went to dances in the town hall. They were from 9 p.m. to 2 p.m. and cost 2s 6d. There were often fights between Air Force and Army personnel. One other vivid memory I have is of lots of Poles arriving. They were refugees and had special housing built for them in Balnageith.

In 1943, at eighteen, I joined the WAAFs. My teenage experiences of the war are very different to those who lived in more built-up, targeted areas.

Ethel Mary Lewis

When the war with Germany started on 3 September 1939, I was nearly fourteen years old. I lived in Camberwell, South-East London, with my family. I lived with Mum, Dad, my sister, brother-in-law, and nephew. My other two sisters had already left home. One was married and the other had joined the ATS.

I was evacuated with the school to Pulborough in Sussex and was billeted with a Mr and Mrs Russell. It was awful having to leave my family as I was so worried about them still being in London, and there was the fear that our house would be bombed and I would never see them again. My nephew Derek also came with me to Pulborough, as he was three years younger than me. We had to walk to school every day which was a 4-mile round trip. We used to look out for each other—that's what people did. As we were so close in age he was more like a baby brother to me than a nephew.

Mr and Mrs Russell were nice people. They lived in a nice house just outside the village—in fact, it's still there. From their house you could see the Chanctonbury Ring. This is a copse of trees on the South Downs. I was told that the fairies danced around it. It was very pretty. I later learnt that Bertrand Russell once said, 'any view that includes Chanctonbury Ring is a good view,' so I felt extremely lucky!

Jean Green

I was seven-and-a-quarter years old in September 1939. Before war was officially declared, I remember the issue of gas masks from school. After being shown how to use them, we were expected to take them to school each Friday for a practise. I can't recall being alarmed at this procedure, more amused, and I can still remember the distinctive rubber smell around my face.

I lived in Plymouth at the outbreak of the Second World War and was still not particularly aware of the ramifications of this event.

Rationing didn't play any big part in my life until when I went away to school, but more of that later.

We lived in an upper rented flat in a small terraced house with a back garden. The air-raid shelter was there and I have many memories of it. Once the air-raids began in 1940, my mother (always a practical soul) would religiously take a feast of cocoa, biscuits, and any other available snacks down in preparation for the air-raids each evening. We used the shelter regularly. I had a special outfit for when the siren went, usually at night. These were a pair of 'slacks', a jumper, and thick coat which went over my pyjamas. I can even now remember the routine of putting on this outfit, and it became almost a nightly way of life. We shared this air-raid shelter with our downstairs neighbours, the Prews, who had two children. As children we were often sorry when the 'all-clear' sounded, as we would be playing many guessing games. The only occasions on which we seemed to be scared was when told to duck as *they* were coming over—'*they*' being enemy aircraft, often the closest of bombs landing with immense noise.

The best use of this shelter when not on alert was by me organising concerts for the other kids in the street. I would produce, direct, and star in many shows where we merrily sang songs like 'Happy days are here again' and 'Sons of the old contemptibles', of which we had no understanding.

We took everything in our stride and still went off to school (always walking of course) each day without a bother.

Regarding food, our power was often non-existent and I can remember my mother cooking in a biscuit tin on the coal fire. Although I cannot remember much of what we had to eat, I do recall never being hungry.

We were eventually bombed out, which meant we moved to another upstairs rented flat. By this time I was nine and sat my scholarship at nine and a half, being quite a bright child. I passed this exam and in the September was evacuated to Truro, as this was the only way I could accept my grammar school place. I loved this way of life and took to it like a duck to water, despite all the voluble doubts of various members of the family who had always considered me a spoilt only child. Dormitory life was great. We were housed in part of the nuns' accommodation attached to Truro Cathedral. As imaginative young girls this gave us great cause for 'seeing ghosts'. Apart from food, where our diets were boring and not very nice with lumpy porridge, horrible stringy meat and pretty grim vegetables, we were happy. We were blessed with desserts of apples in every shape from the orchard nearby.

While away at school war life hardly touched us, but at the end of each term when we came home, we were once again made very aware of the war. Plymouth City was virtually bombed to the ground. My parents had again been bombed out and, although I can't remember exactly when, were moved to yet another rented upstairs flat.

My mother worked through the war in Timothy White's hardware store. My father was employed by the Post Office in a reserved occupation, mostly at night, and although I don't know for certain, I was given the impression that he worked in a secret communication office underground.

Whenever I was at home, I can remember how religiously the blackout was observed with thick, heavy-duty curtains.

One very vivid memory is of when I was very ill with a mastoid infection, during which time I had a very high temperature. I was too ill to go to the air-raid shelter, and my mother and I crouched under the stairs so that I couldn't go out and get a cold. Ironically this coincided with particularly heavy bombing, which I believe was connected with the oil refineries at Plymouth being bombed. The fires from these illuminated the city and helped enemy bombers find their targets.

The radio played a huge part in our lives. Every bulletin was religiously listened to and paid due respect. Cheers erupted every time reports of British successes against Germany were announced.

When the war ended, like everyone in the country, we children were very happy but there remained little niggles of regret that our school returned to Plymouth and we were no longer boarders.

21

Ruth Abbey (née Jackson)

I was nine years old when war broke out on 3 September 1939, but I soon turned ten on the 26th. I had a sister, Olive, eighteen months older than me. Although I was called Ruth, my Sunday name was 'Winifred'.

I was evacuated with my mother to Bilsthorpe in Nottingham for a very short while to stay with an auntie. We hated it so much we had the fare sent to us to come home, back to Colchester.

I remember the night-time air-raids very well. The windows were taped and black out curtain blinds were put up. If there was even a chink of light the air-raid warden would knock heavily on the door to remind you to close them up properly.

We were supplied with a Morrison shelter which was a table shelter, but we never used it.

If there was an air-raid at night we did not have to arrive at school until 10 a.m. the following morning. When the sirens went during the school hours we were assembled and went down to the school's air-raid shelter.

Children had to have emergency rations at school in case they were necessary having to spend a long time in the shelters.

At the age of fourteen I went to work as a trainee accountant. Some Saturday nights, with two others, we would have to spend the night fire watching. All the many buildings had to be unlocked (with only the aid of a small torch) and then relocked in the morning.

As I only earned 10s a week (minus 4d's insurance) and paid my mother 7s the extra money from fire-watching (3s and 9d), my week's money came to 6s and 5d. This was most welcome.

We lived close to Colchester Barracks, so while these were still being made habitable for the troops, we were asked whether we would take any soldiers in. They were Australian soldiers and we would receive a knock on the door asking how many we could take. Much the same as when evacuees were being placed, we had two soldiers staying with us in the front room. They didn't stay long as the barracks were soon ready for them.

I remember I could always hear the barracks band playing in the evenings—'Bugler Rang' and 'Lights Out'—and I would find it hard to get to sleep.

When war ended there were great celebrations in the town hall and at the park on Holly Trees lawn, where the school children sang 'Pomp and Circumstance'. The Oxford and Bucks Band played, with Colonel Needham conducting 'Land of Hope and Glory' and 'All men must be free'.

We had a street party in Kendal Road with trestle tables to sit and eat at, and bunting hanging from the houses. The German POWs choir and our choir sang. On Sunday evening there would be refreshments for the troops and dancing on the Holly Trees lawn. Two prayers that would be said were 'Bless this house, O Lord we pray' and 'Remember them, those far-away'.

22

Christopher J. Pengelly

I wasn't born until 1935, so I do not remember much of the war until 1940 when my father was called up. I remember him saying goodbye to my mother and me. I recall us both crying; we were obviously very upset.

I always thought rationing was the normal thing at that time. It wasn't until I was a little older that I came to appreciate the things that we missed.

We had a shelter just opposite the house where we lived, which was very convenient. We went in there quite often during the Blitz of Exeter and Exmouth. Exmouth, even though it was a smallish town, suffered quite badly. This was mostly due to its proximity to Exeter. The Germans would discard their bombs over the area on their way back to Germany.

Life to me in the shelter was quite exciting. Playing with the other children and being able to stay up late at night, although the noise was a little frightening, was a novelty.

We had an evacuee staying with us called Elsie. All I can remember of her was that she arrived with fleas and smelt of mothballs. My mother was quite concerned. I know on certain occasions, when one of our relations came to stay, I had to sleep with her—an experience never forgotten. She actually came to visit my mother in the '60s; she was married and had quite a few children.

The special events during the war were going home to my grandmother's and granddad's home in Lyme Regis. That was my mother's home town. I know I was always spoilt when I was there. The journey was also exciting as we went by train, which was quite an event and something new.

We went to Lyme Regis for Christmas and special occasions. Any excuse to see my cousins on their birthdays and mine.

One of the exciting moments I can remember of the war was an occasion on which a friend and I were coming home from school one day. We stopped to talk to two soldiers who were manning a twin-barrelled gun on a mobile carrier. You could go inside and sit in the turret, which was very exciting for a boy.

While we were there five or six planes came over. The soldiers shouted out, 'They're Germans, get inside.' My friend was pushed inside and I was pushed under the van, but being very nosey I looked out to see what was going on. I saw the planes flying very low and I could see the pilots very plainly. They were flying towards the sea and the gun was firing at them, two lines of tracer bullets, all of which were missing the tails of the planes. I can remember saying to myself, fire in front of them, you'll hit them then. I wasn't stupid, even at eight years old.

I was all over very quickly as they were flying too fast. I know at the time it was quite exciting, but looking back now, it could have been a little different, especially if they had turned around and decided to attack the gun we were in.

I can also remember the bombing of Exmouth. Two raids were severe and caused many casualties. One of these was German planes dropping their bombs on their way home. The other was on the docks, as there were a lot of coal ships there which supplied Exeter and other nearby towns.

For a small town we did not come off well. The devastation we witnessed going into Exmouth after a raid was very alarming. I just couldn't believe it.

I can remember the war ending; all the street parties that took place, everyone enjoying themselves—such a happy time.

There were also sad times; many of my friends had lost their fathers, killed in the war. We were the lucky ones. My father was only wounded; he went to Normandy, but was brought home after only spending a week out there. He did recover well, though. I didn't see my father after that until 1948; he had to go to Palestine for three years to help with the troubles out there.

Kes Cole

Although the family home was in Manor Park, in 1943, aged seven, I found myself as an evacuee. I was staying with my paternal grandparents in the old alms houses in Colchester. To me, the sun always seemed to shine, it seldom rained, and Colchester was a whole planet away from the war and the bombs that my parents were dodging back home in the Blitz. In East London, my Dad managed a workshop in Barking maintaining a fleet of battleship grey POOL petrol supply tankers.

Granddad Cole was a lovely old man; although bald he had a fringe of snow-white hair and a short clipped moustache. He smoked St Julian tobacco in his pipe and he always seemed to have time for me. I never recall him losing his temper. We would play cards by the fire, games like 'Snap' or 'drain the well dry'. He would invent games; one being two bits of firewood tied together with some of Nan's knitting wool. This was our 'fishing tackle', and we would sit for ages trying to catch fish from the coal scuttle.

I had never seen a banana, orange, or any nut other than a cob nut, which could be found along the local hedgerows. Practically everything was rationed or non-existent. Home-grown fruit was used to make jam. I remember having a birthday party with fish paste sandwiches and cone wafers filled with thick egg custard instead of expensive ice-cream. Bananas were hand-made from mashed up boiled parsnips and banana essence. Food during this time held no appeal and I would rather be out playing. One day Nan had an idea and baked me Yorkshire pudding, giving it to me with butter and sugar. The hot pud melted the butter and blended with the sugar. I thought it was gorgeous.

During this time with my grandparents, the bombs of London were a distant memory until Mum visited and reminded us of their hardships.

When the war ended I was aged nine and living back in Manor Park. I felt I had learned a lot, especially a lifelong respect and admiration for the countryside.

Susan Kerr

I was born in Colchester in July 1934 and during the Second World War lived at 'Meadowcroft', Rectory Hill, Wivenhoe. Wivenhoe is a village on the River Colne where shipbuilding, fishing, and agriculture provided the main employment.

My father, being a master butcher, with several shops in the nearby towns, was in a 'reserved occupation' and not called up into the armed services. I was very lucky that my parents were at home during the war years. My father was in the local Home Guard and joined the Royal Observer Corps which had premises in Colchester, so felt he had made some contribution to the war effort. My family were fortunate in that we were never short of meat, and as we kept chickens had plenty of eggs, too. Fruit and vegetables were available due to the 'dig for victory' campaign. Of course the produce was local and seasonal, and I didn't see a banana for years. I well remember going to the local shop where we could buy just ONE orange and the shopkeeper saying, 'That's the last orange you will have until the war is over.'

There was a great deal of ration swapping. My family never used all their tea ration, so tea was swapped with another family's supplies. The Wivenhoe policeman during the war years had two big teenage sons who were always hungry, so some of our cheese ration went to that family.

The wartime diet, though limited, was very healthy and children had concentrated orange juice provided for them. We also had cousins in British Columbia who sent us food parcels during this time, which was a treat. Tinned butter, tinned sock-eye salmon from the Fraser River, maple syrup products, sweets I think, and I believe dried vine fruit.

As for clothing, that was in short supply too. Families passed on outgrown children's clothes to each other. Worn adult's cloths were cut down to make children's garments and hand-knitted woollens were unravelled, washed to remove the 'kinks' in the wool, and knitted up again into children's jumpers and cardigans. My grandmother knitted gloves, mittens, and socks for me. I didn't much like these hand-knitted clothes; being very fair-skinned I found them very itchy and scratchy, but no use complaining—they kept me warm.

My first very vivid memory of the war was of the day it was declared. I was in the back garden watching my father and three or four other men digging our underground shelter. My mother must have had the wireless (as it was known then) on in the house. She came rushing out of the back door screaming, 'we are at war'.

Although efforts were made to make our underground air-raid shelter comfortable with camp beds, a little table, and a chair, it was always cold and damp, the walls streaming with condensation. This moisture ran into a sump at the bottom of the entry steps; frogs were the only creatures who happily lived there. It was a great relief when a Morrison shelter was installed in the living room in the house. This was a large brown painted metal table with mesh sides. We had a mattress and blankets under this table, so it was fairly comfortable, though it did take up a lot space and had very sharp edges which I can remember bumping into when playing.

I started school at Grey Friars on East Hill, Colchester, when I was five years old. My Aunty Mary was secretary at the school so took me to and from there on the bus from Wivenhoe. I enjoyed school right from the start, but it was soon temporarily closed while underground air-raid shelters were constructed in the grounds. However, education continued in my own home. Girls from Wivenhoe and neighbouring villages came and sat round my dining table for lessons given by visiting teachers. Once back at school, we were put through rigorous drills of filing out of our classrooms when the air-raid siren sounded and, complete with gas mask (which went everywhere with us), we went down into the underground shelter. There were benches around the walls which like my shelter at home were damp with condensation. My mother made me a little brown velvet cushion to take to the shelter so I didn't have to lean against the damp concrete. Our teachers did their best to keep us happy by singing songs, 'One man went to Mow' and 'Ten Green Bottles hanging on the wall'. Luckily, in spite of being an Army town, Colchester was not heavily bombed, so I never felt frightened down the shelter.

The town of Colchester was always (and still is) full of soldiers being a garrison town. Those recovering from war wounds at the military hospital wore a special light blue uniform so were very obvious. One clear memory was of a hot summer day when a platoon of soldiers was resting under the shade of trees on a bank opposite my home. My mother felt sorry for them, they looked hot and tired, so told me to take a box of cigarettes across to offer them. I felt very shy and didn't want to do this but my mother persuaded me.

As well as the barracks in Colchester there was also an Army camp in the grounds of Wivenhoe Park, so I was used to seeing soldiers in Wivenhoe. These were soldiers of the Commonwealth and Allied forces on R&R. There was a scheme run, I think, by the padre of the camp whereby two soldiers visited local families for tea on a Sunday afternoon. My parents entertained Canadian, Polish, and Czech soldiers, and many became lifelong friends. I am still in touch with two Canadian families whose father or grandfather visited my parents during the war.

The Canadians taught me to ice-skate on a local lake during a bitterly cold winter (I think in 1943) and after the war sent me a pair of very glamorous white skating boots from Canada. The Polish soldiers made me an iced cake for my birthday, a luxury unheard of during the war years. The Czech soldiers fixed me up with a pen friend who I wrote to for years after the war was over.

The only downside to the closeness of so many soldiers was the danger attracted by Army vehicles and tanks on the roads. When visiting the local shop with my mother's help, we were nearly run down by a tank which skidded when taking a corner too sharply. A scary moment! We both ran and flung ourselves on the ground out of its way. I also met American service men at a social club, run I think by the Red Cross, in Colchester. My Aunty Mary volunteered at this club and sometimes took me there. Even as a small girl I realised how very different the Americans were from us. Very polite, friendly, and much more smartly dressed. I remember one American gave me an apple from his pocket, large and crisp. What a luxury.

My Aunty Mary was a busy lady with the full-time job as the school secretary; looking after my grandmother (a role unmarried daughters were expected to fill); and 'fire watching' on the roof of the school at night on a rota system. This was the only time in her life my Aunty ever wore trousers.

There were POWs in this area working on farms. The local people accepted them, just young men caught up in the war; no hatred apparent on either side. Several of the men met local girls and married them after the war and stayed in the area as respected members of the community.

My godfather, Wilf Hodgson, was the sanitary inspector for Wivenhoe Council. He was called up with the Royal Army Medical Corps. A great friend of my parents, he kept in touch all through the war and spent some of his service leave with my family. When he was on active service abroad all letters home to England were censored, large areas blacked out. I think they were also photographed because the letters arrived on a different sort of paper, not ordinary writing paper. On one leave, my parents and my godfather worked out a very simple code so he could tell them where he was when abroad. The first letter of each sentence would spell out the location. The censors must have been very dim not to figure that out when CAIRO was so obvious. My godfather brought me back some lovely presents from his overseas service. A filigree silver bracelet from Egypt featuring pyramids and camels; also from the Middle East a little book, *Flowers of the Holy Land*, pressed wild flowers in olive wood covers.

There were evacuees, although my family did not take any. I was very friendly with a pretty and nice evacuee called Ann Rivers who was staying nearby. We never kept in touch, but I often think of her.

As the war dragged on, life took on a routine. 'Take your gas mask with you,' 'what is your National Identity Number?' My parents made sure I never forgot my National Identity Number in case I ever became separated from them in a crisis. I also wore a little silver disc on a silver chain round my neck with my name engraved on it.

Children being what they are, I still had fun in spite of the war. I watched British and German planes having dog fights high in the blue summery skies—that was exciting. The next morning I would hunt for shrapnel in the garden; the kids would compete with each other as to who had the biggest shrapnel collection. I also picked up thin strips of aluminium which was scattered from British planes to disturb and disrupt radar signals. In the dull days of war, these could be made into decorations. From my garden I could also see barrage balloons protecting radio masts in the area.

Another great find was the jettisoned fuel tanks which returning British planes would release before landing. East Anglia had many small airfields, so these were plentiful. They were about 6 to 8 feet long, cigar-shaped metal tanks with a square cut into them—a canoe was made. My parents strictly forbade me to play in these canoes on the tidal River Colne—quite rightly. Only the older boys from the fishing families who were as home on the water as they were on dry land could do that. However, there were several small fresh-water ponds, only knee-deep in the fields behind my home and I would play there.

I can remember looking up and seeing the sky full of planes in formation. Later we learned that that was D-Day, 6 June 1944.

In 1944, we saw the V1 rockets (doodlebugs) streaking across the horizon with a trail of flames behind them. We held our breath, for once the rocket stopped (and it was noisy), it would fall to earth and destroy whatever it hit, sometimes with great loss of life. My brother, William, was born in July 1944. My mother called him her doodlebug baby.

The local shipyards had a part to play in D-Day, building landing craft and sections of the Mulberry Harbour on the marshes. Of course, the residents didn't know what all the extra activity and noise at the shipyard was all about, only later was the story told. Civilians made use of cast-off military items; wedding dresses and bridesmaid dresses were made of parachute silk, and my mother had a nightie made out of it too for the birth of my baby brother. The silk-printed navigation maps made wonderful headscarves—the list is endless.

Overall, I was not frightened during the war. The worse moment was early in 1944, when my mother, pregnant with my brother, was resting on the sofa in the living room. I was playing nearby when we saw through the window approaching rapidly and on fire—an aeroplane. My mother rolled off the sofa and tried to make a dive for the Morrison shelter, thinking the blazing plane would hit the house. By great good luck, it skimmed over the roof and crashed into the fields behind the house. Many of the villagers and especially the children wanted to see the crashed plane, a German fighter aircraft. The local police and air-raid wardens mounted a guard to keep sightseers away. Later that evening, the children (including myself) crept back. The smell of burned metal and wiring was very strong and the plane, a total wreck. The kids climbed over, on, and into the wreckage. The body of the pilot must have been removed, but I picked up his flight log book and took it home. My father was quietly angry and said, 'You better give that to me.' I never saw it again. Presumably my father handed it to the authorities so the plane and pilot could be identified.

Eventually peacetime came when I was eleven years old and at secondary school in Colchester. There was a street party in our area to celebrate. Long tables were laid with food and drink on a piece of waste ground. How the housewives managed to provide such a spread to celebrate on rationing, I do not know.

The war years of my childhood have certainly influenced my character; I still have my 3 inches of bath water (a requirement during war time, fuel was too scare to waste heating up water for a deep bath). I feel uncomfortable with any sort of waste—food, paper, and clothing. I still save little pieces of string. I am an enthusiastic re-cycler; I have always done it, the younger generation think it is their idea—Oh no! I also relish all the imported fruit, unlimited sweets and chocolate, plus travel in this country or abroad, as there were no holidays in war time.

25

Barry Lewis (Lucioni)

One may think that for an eighty year old to remember the events of seventy odd years ago would be a big ask, but by some freak of nature, and in common with many of my generation, the events of the 1940s are clearer in my mind, than the events of last month. I can clearly remember the declaration of war, a lovely sunny Sunday morning, five days before my sixth birthday, I was sitting on our door step singing happily, my Dad was taking a bath in our downstairs bathroom when he suddenly stopped me in mid-refrain, because there was an announcement on the radio—the declaration by Neville Chamberlain that we were at war with Germany. The gravity of the situation was of course largely lost on a blissfully happy child of six, but the concern that suddenly appeared in the faces and voices of my Mum and Dad was palpable, and I could sense that major changes were about to take place—an intuition that manifested itself almost immediately when the previously unknown word 'evacuation' suddenly entered our lives. Just one week later we were part of a contingent of children bound for Adderbury, in Oxfordshire. The 'we' referred to were my sister Frances and me—she was fourteen months older—and my brother Tony, who was sixteen months younger and was deemed too young for this venture.

We coped quite well in Adderbury, the first time away from our parents, but it was something of a failed experiment and we were all back home for Christmas. Life in Dagenham was bliss; we were totally untroubled by the fact that there was a war on, until evacuation became the topic of conversation again, and by June of 1940 we were on our way to Devon, this time with Tony and three cousins. Under normal circumstances a group of six wouldn't have been a problem, but we were the descendants of an adventurous Italian who had left his homeland a century earlier to make his home in London, and now we were at war with Italy, sporting the very Italian name of Lucioni. When we descended on the tiny Hamlet of Uplowman in deepest Devon, the reaction of the locals ranged between discomfort and aggression, which I have to say was short-lived. The two years that we spent there were some of the happiest of our lives, and in 2010 the good people of Uplowman invited us back for a seventieth anniversary reunion.

Brother Tony and I were billeted with a Bert Saunders, who was a farm labourer for the local squire. He supplemented this living with a bit of part-time poaching and scrumping, the art of which he was happy to pass on to me, and at eight years old I was able to set a snare, catch a rabbit, and identify any tree or bird that I ever encountered. When we had to be re-billeted because of Mrs Saunders's impending addition to her family, we moved 100 yards up the street to the Shorts, whose smallholding included goats, beehives, ducks, geese, *etc.*, all of which I took to wholeheartedly. Leaving Uplowman was a sad day; we were missing Mum, who was on her own because of Dad's posting to Germany.

Our third and final taste of evacuation was to North Wales, which to our young minds was almost abroad. Holywell in Flintshire was not a happy experience for me. I was happy with my hosts who were farmers, and extremely well off, and the experience I had acquired in Devon stood me in good stead. Mr Davis (my host) kept three Shire horses, two entirely for work and the younger one for work and shows. I was elected to accompany Prince into the show ground and felt a million miles from my Dagenham home, but the biggest thrill I had was to ride one of the huge Shire horses while trailing the other one behind me as some of the friends who had come with me from Dagenham looked on enviously. I felt like I was born to this life, but there was a fly in the ointment: during the gap between Devon and North Wales, I had sat the Eleven Plus Exam. Although only ten and a half, I had passed it, so on arriving in North Wales, I was enrolled at the Hollywell County School, the flagship of the Flintshire education system. The main drawback for me was that the school was 80-per-cent Welsh-speaking, a disadvantage that I may have come to terms with, but such was the pride of the staff in their education standard that they were determined to show the Essex system of which I was a product in as bad a light as possible. Of course, they were doing all this in a language of which I was completely ignorant; even at this late stage I cannot forgive them, because I am convinced that their actions changed the course of my life, and spoilt what could have been an extremely happy time for me. On the spur of the moment I decided to come home; I placed my pet kitten in a cardboard box, and latched onto a friend's parents who had come to take him home. I questioned the wisdom of the move when having boarded an underground train after arriving in Paddington; the train was halted outside East Ham because gunfire and bombs were all around us. I saw the rest of the war out with just my mother; my father was still in Germany, my sister and brother still in North Wales. I saw plenty of sad happenings but was most cut up when my teacher informed me that Peter Tiffin, the bespectacled little Yorkshire kid who sat next to me, would no longer be doing so, as his house had taken a direct hit the night before and there were no survivors.

Our first period of evacuation was almost certainly the saddest, because we missed the routine of playing in familiar streets and running up the street to meet our Dad coming home from work. Probably the hardest time was bedtime.

For some strange reason it seems that I was born with a strong belief in God, and I can remember praying fervently for the safety of not only my nearest and dearest, but of almost everyone that I knew and liked. As I have already said, Uplowman turned out to be an absolute delight. I should mention here the teachers: a Miss Paignton travelled with us from our Dagenham School and was an absolute angel; we ran to her with all our problems both real and imagined. Also the head teacher of Uplowman School, Miss Yeoman, who took to me immediately and was a great comfort and help the whole time we were there. The Lucionis settled into their new life. We did suffer a bit of resentment from the village kids, and our oldest cousin Teddy, who was twelve, was often called to fight our corner—a role that stood him in good stead, as he later became a professional boxer and won his first twenty-two fights by knock outs. Within a few weeks of arriving, Billy and I were singing in the Church choir and Teddy was pumping the organ. I can clearly recall Christmas at the Saunders's: Tony and I shared a bed and we were discussing the likelihood of Santa Claus having been informed of our whereabouts. As the older brother, I was trying to prepare Tony for the worst without being too brutal. I can still remember the relief and wonder when we awoke to find a cowboy hat and guns, a small tin of paints each, a colouring book, an orange, a couple of walnuts, and a small jar of sweets—even now, almost eighty Christmases since, this still stands out as one of the best.

26

Maria Barella (née Bizzanelli)

My father was born in Garzeno, a small village above Lake Como in Italy, in 1911. My grandmother came back to the UK shortly before the outbreak of the First World War, leaving my father to be brought up by his grandparents. My grandfather had a restaurant in Herne Hill, South-East London, where a number of other Italians also had various eateries. My father then joined the rest of his family here when he was twelve. By then he had four sisters who he had never met, and was sent to school with no understanding of English.

At some point my father travelled back to Italy to continue a friendship with my mother, who he brought over to the UK and married in 1933. Before the outbreak of the Second World War he bought his first café, and they worked very hard together to make it a success. At the outbreak of the war with Italy in the 1940s, they experienced some prejudice from a small minority and subsequently my father was interned on the Isle of Man (thankfully not sent to Canada).

My mother, with very poor English, was left to run the café with a little help from my aunts (who were still quite young); the majority of her English neighbours and customers were very supportive. Bus conductors and their drivers when finishing shifts would pop by to see if she needed help locking up, and should there be an air-raid, neighbours and other business owners would check up on her and accompany her to the shelters. Even the local policemen stopped by on their beat to see if she was alright.

Very frequently she would go to the police and various offices that dealt with the internees and plead for my father's release. It was on one of these occasions that she met with another Italian lady and her family pleading for her husband's release too. They went on to have a lifetime's friendship. I believe my father was interned for almost two years, and it was after his release that my mother fell pregnant with me. It seems that before the war they had looked into adoption, and in 1943 I was born.

My earliest and vivid memory is of sitting under a tree in Brockwell Park and seeing my father running with his bicycle up the hill towards us under the tree and looking up to the sky to see what was happening. It was some sort of bomb—probably the silent one—and he dropped the bike and ran to be with us under the tree. Obviously, I recall only the scene and was later told the facts. I was probably only between eighteen months or two years old, but I can still picture it, such was the terror of my parents at that moment.

1. Family photo with siblings. (*Joy Blackmur*)

2. Joy Blackmur during the Second World War. (*Joy Blackmur*)

3. Vivian Sherry aged fifteen. (*Vivian Sherry*)

4. With my mother aged four. (*Vivian Sherry*)

5. Sitting on the coach. (*Ethel Lewis*)

6. Our billet. (*Ethel Lewis*)

7. Wood Farm, where we were evacuated. (*Elizabeth Kemble*)

8. Extended family outing to the seaside. (*Elizabeth Kemble*)

9. Dad digging the shelter. (*Elizabeth Kemble*)

10. Older siblings dressed for work. (*Elizabeth Kemble*)

Above : 11. Isabelle and friend Doris with their bicycles aged fourteen. (*Isabelle Alexander*)

Right: 12. Me and my Dad. (*Angela Aston*)

Below left: 13. Angela Aston. (*Angela Aston*)

Below right: 14. Maria wearing the dress made from parachute silk. (*Maria Barella*)

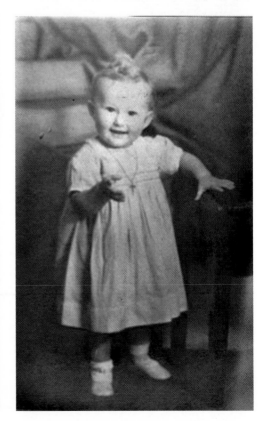

15. Garzeno Church, where the officer hid. (*Ugo Barella*)

16. Barella House, now derelict, where they lived during the Second World War. (*Ugo Barella*)

17. A Barella family photo. (*Ugo Barella*)

18. My dad and I. (*Maureen Timby*)

19. Our air-raid shelter. (*Robert Welham*)

20. Mum and me at Wanstead Flats pond. (*Robert Welham*)

21. Pamela Taylor, eight-and-a-half years old, in Wales. (*Pamela Drummond*)

DEAR MUMMY.
THANK YOU FOR THE
PARCEL AND LETTER
I AM BEING A GOOD
GIRL I made a hipbd
send me a letter wen
you like I've got a baled
Lots OF LOVE AND
KISSES AND A BIG
HUG FROM BRENDA
XXXXXXXXXXXXXX

22. Letter from Brenda to Mum. (*George Osborn*)

23. George's sketch of Aunty Annie's House. (*George Osborn*)

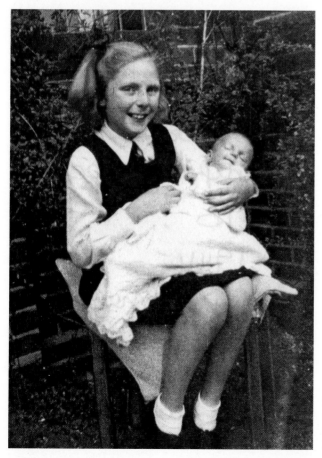

24. Susan in school uniform aged ten with William, my 'doodlebug' baby brother, born in 1944. (*Susan Kerr*)

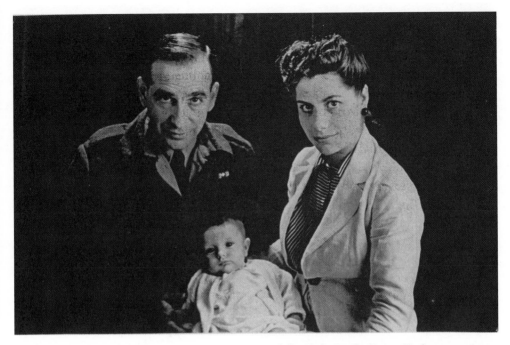

25. Andy Hamel with his English wife, Violet, and their baby Linda. (*Susan Kerr*)

26. Father, mother, and myself in the
summer of 1942. (*Susan Kerr*)

27. Peter at nursery school during a music session, middle-front with tambourine. (*Rose Aitken-Smith*)

28. Pam and Terry. (*Pam and Terry Woods*)

29. Barbara and her father.
(*Barbara Harvey*)

30. My parents just after I was born.
(*Barbara Harvey*)

31. My father in his uniform.
(*Barbara Harvey*)

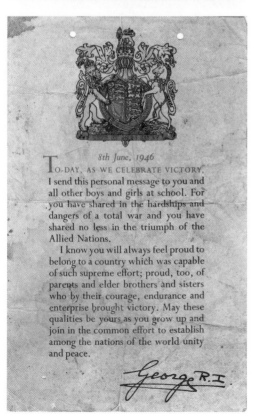

8th June, 1946

TO-DAY, AS WE CELEBRATE VICTORY, I send this personal message to you and all other boys and girls at school. For you have shared in the hardships and dangers of a total war and you have shared no less in the triumph of the Allied Nations.

I know you will always feel proud to belong to a country which was capable of such supreme effort; proud, too, of parents and elder brothers and sisters who by their courage, endurance and enterprise brought victory. May these qualities be yours as you grow up and join in the common effort to establish among the nations of the world unity and peace.

George R.I.

32. Thank you letter from the King sent to all children in 1946.

Sweets and confectionary ranged from very scarce to non-existent, and my mother would guard any that she had fiercely. When we had to go on a bus journey she would pass one to the bus conductor, and when he came to sell us the tickets he would give me a sweet—well, did I love going on buses?

My mother was very careful with money and inventive with food, as well as making most of mine and her clothing. One dress in particular was made with parachute material; this was after the war, when material was scarce.

Jan Gearon-Simm

I was born in 1941. One of our family's stories of that time was that the bombs had dislodged tiles from the roof of our council house in Dagenham, as well as from the roofs of our neighbours' houses. Everyone except my Dad had retreated to the Anderson shelters in their back gardens. Even though the overhead planes were dropping their deadly cargoes, my Dad took his ladder from the garage and propped it up against the wall of our house, having picked up whole tiles beforehand and then replaced them on our roof. He later said the tiles were not marked as belonging to any particular house, so he had no qualms about what he was doing. Although he was an honest man in peacetime, he felt that, in war, it was sometimes essential to behave in ways that were less than honourable but necessary at the time.

My mother was hard of hearing and, if she was indoors, she often did not hear the sirens warning residents of approaching bomb-dropping planes. Our neighbours took responsibility for making sure she was out of the house and in the shelter until the all-clear signal was heard. My mother was a positive person, and remarked that she had had a very relaxed war because her hearing was deficient.

My father told us that, at the start of a bombing raid, he once overheard his neighbour next door yelling to his wife to come back to their shelter. On her way back to their house, she yelled that she had forgotten her false teeth, to which he replied angrily, 'They're not dropping bloody sandwiches!'

G. Lewis

We lived in Reede Road, Dagenham. Just after the war started we were evacuated. We all had to meet at Hunter's Hall School with a few clothes. We were then taken by bus to Dagenham Dock to catch a Paddle Steamer to Gorleston near Great Yarmouth. After spending the night in a school sleeping on straw, the next day we were put on another bus to take us to a place called Wickmere School, in Norfolk. We had to line up and people took their pick. There were three of us, my brother, my sister, and me. We were the last to go. Nobody wanted three. We went to a lovely couple, a gamekeeper and his wife who had a nice house in the middle of a field. We had no running water or electricity. We stayed for about six months and then we all got sent to Staffordshire, where we stayed for about two months and then returned to Dagenham.

Our family had a shelter in the garden where we went every night. Our gas masks smelt of rubber. We were in Dagenham when the Battle of Britain was on. I then went back to Norfolk on my own to live with the gamekeeper and his wife. Mr and Mrs Newstead had sent for me. He was gamekeeper to Lord and Lady Walpole and the grounds where I was living was Wolterton Hall. We had a pump in the kitchen for water, and a range cooker where we boiled water for a tin bath in the kitchen.

We had an oil lamp in the lounge and went to bed with a candle. We had about a 5-mile walk to school the first time we had stayed, but when I went back on my own I went to the village school. It was nice and Mrs Baker was the teacher. An Army camp was built in the woods and I had to walk through this every day to get to school.

We lived about 17 miles from Norwich and watched a bomb drop from the front door. While I was there I went shooting with the gamekeeper and had a .22 rifle. I worked in the gardens of the hall so I could buy a bike. The boys at school had a carpentry lesson at Aylsham, which was about 7 miles away, and we went over on our bikes once a week. I was upset when my father went away and my brother got called up at the same time. After the war I went back to Norfolk seven years running, as I liked to see the people I lived with and my school friends.

I left school at Christmas 1945 and went to work in Stepney to be a bricklayer. All the work was on houses with bomb damage.

Marian Bull

I was ten when my father drove me up to Taunton to stay with a cousin for a fortnight. He put a 10-*s* note on the mantelpiece with the instructions that I was to be put on the first train home if war was declared. He arrived to fetch me on the following Sunday morning. As we crossed the railway bridge by Churston Station on the way home, he saw two workmen carrying their gas masks. Tears rolled down my father's cheeks as he said, 'That means we're at war.'

Within the week we went to the Sunday school to collect our gas masks. They smelt of rubber and at first it was frightening—it seemed impossible to breathe. The ladies who were fitting them placed a piece of card under the snout and told you to breathe in: if it was a good fit the card stayed there. It didn't take long for us to discover how to make rude farting noises with them.

We lived over the shop in the main street. There were storerooms behind the shop where my father stored the fishermen's oilskins, which were one of the things he sold in his clothing business. These items were moved elsewhere, as these storerooms were deemed to be the safest place in the event of air-raids. The first time that I ever felt real fear was when I saw my father preparing it and realised that I might be in danger. There were many more times before the war was over when I was truly frightened. We had a couple of straw-filled paillasses there to sit and lie on and a chair for mother. It was quite a trek going down two flights of stairs and then about 20 yards through part of the shop to get there. We took a circuitous route, as there was a glass skylight over part of the shop. The first thing we always did was boil the kettle on a little methylated spirit stove and make the inevitable cup of tea. Sometimes the air-raid siren would sound three or more times in the night, and after trekking up and down several times we would decide to stay there.

During the bombing of Exeter and Plymouth the planes would cross our part of the coast. They would drone overhead in waves for what seemed like hours. Eventually we could hear them returning, and there were occasions when they dropped their remaining bombs on the way back. Once, a stick of incendiaries was dropped but quickly dealt with. We had our own stirrup pump and practised with buckets of water in the back yard. Large water tanks were put at various places around the town to be used if the mains water was out of action.

In 1940 I started attending Torquay Girls Grammar School and travelling by train. After one particularly bad night of bombs I could hear the rhythm of the train chanting, 'We have been bombed, we have been bombed.'

After heavy raids up-country and with troop trains on the move, our train home would often be very late. We would sit on the station platform knowing that there was no excuse for homework not done, no matter how late we got home. Yet I can't remember anyone grumbling—we accepted everything that we had to endure.

My father was in the Special Police. On one occasion he was called to a bungalow in a part of town not far away. Something had crashed through the roof and couldn't be identified. Dad had been investigating this lump of metal and apparently debating what it might be, as it was known that scrap metal had been used in the foundations. Luckily there was a soldier from the newly formed bomb disposal squad on leave nearby and he was called in for his advice. He knew immediately that it was a time bomb. The people living nearest to it were evacuated and some came to us. At 6.00 a.m. in the morning it went off, windows were shattered over a wide area including some of ours.

It was in the early summer of 1940 that I was sitting by our beach hut on Breakwater Beach. A flotilla of strange looking fishing boats began chugging into Brixham Harbour. There was furniture stacked on the decks and women and children standing around the bows looking curiously at the approaching harbour. They were all met on arrival and empty properties found to house them. They were Belgian refugees. The bakers were called out to bake a batch of bread for all the newcomers. The men were sent in their boats around the coast to South Wales (I think) to be vetted as they would soon be going out fishing with chances to communicate with the enemy, overnight fishing was not allowed.

I was in the top class of the school and was given the task of teaching a Belgian girl pounds, shillings, and pence with cardboard coins. I also, at my mother's request, gave one of my favourite dolls to a Belgian girl. I'm sure she didn't love her as much as I did.

I think it was at about this time that the evacuees arrived. My father was on duty and the children were brought to a nearby Sunday school. He arrived home to tell my mother that there was a brother and sister who nobody wanted, as the little girl had to wear boots for some sort of trouble with her foot. My family were Methodists and really felt they must do what they could, although our house was officially full. My sister Joan moved into the bed with Eva (my eldest sister) and Helen, and the evacuee shared a bed with me. Billy, her younger brother, shared a bed with my brother David. They were a policeman's children from the Old Kent Road. Helen and I were close in age and had a wonderful time. Soon we were having hit-and-run raids, and at that time London hadn't even been bombed. Their parents decided that they would be safer in London and they went back.

The arrangements for air-raids often changed in the autumn of 1939. At one time we were taken out onto the nearby green and we had to lie flat on the ground. Then we went into the open basement where equipment was stored. When I went on to grammar school the following year we went to various storerooms or under the stage.

I think the idea was for us to get away from the glass. Nothing was reinforced, so that was the only advantage.

There were various air-raids. Lone planes often flew in under the radar and dropped their bombs and disappeared before the siren sounded. An old ship was moored by the Breakwater and used for coal bunkering. One day a lone plane dropped its bomb and sank it. However, since it was moored in shallow water at low tide it appeared to be floating. Twice more a plane spotted it and 'sank' it. We heard Lord Haw-Haw announce on the wireless that a Merchant Ship had been sunk in Brixham Harbour. One morning a bomb was dropped at the end of our road: an off-licence was demolished and one man killed. I was at school and was called to the headmistress to be told that my family were safe.

There was a shipyard which had previously built yachts but was suddenly producing mine sweepers, MTBs, and MGBs. Men who had been in the shipbuilding industry and retired shipwrights returned to work and workers streamed in every day from the surrounding area. A great uncle of mine was on the bridge of an MTB doing the final work after it had been launched. A German plane came in and strafed it; my great uncle was killed outright. On another occasion we heard some bangs and firing at midday on a Sunday. We hurried down to the harbour and saw a newly commissioned minesweeper turn turtle. The crew and their wives, who were being entertained to Sunday lunch, jumped as we watched.

The build-up to D-Day resulted in many changes in the area. Several houses were demolished to allow easier passage for all the various-sized vehicles that embarked on a newly built hard inside the Breakwater. We were not allowed in the area by the embarking site.

Camps were set up in all available spaces. There was one in a field beside our school; the tennis course adjoined it. I was fifteen in 1944 and appreciated the wolf whistles—we all did. It was amazing how often we managed to serve the tennis balls right over the fencing and into the file so that the GIs had to return them. When D-Day arrived, we passed all the vehicles lined up on our way up from the station to the school. They threw us lemons, which we peeled and ate, and chewing gum. Overnight, what had been a camp busy with the noise of vehicles, shouting, constant movement, and smoke from the cookhouse was suddenly deserted and silent. It was eerie, for we knew that they would never return there.

We lived over the shop in the main street on the route to the harbour. For weeks during the preparations manoeuvres were carried out. Long columns of GIs would trudge past for hours to embark by the Breakwater. They wore soft-soled boots and it was eerie to hear voices and see only the flame from a match as they lit a cigarette. Then came convoys of vehicles. I've often thought since how scared they must have been, knowing that many would be killed when it was the real thing.

Scattered around the town in the month before D-Day were small machines that made smoke screens. They were set off without warning so that the whole area was enveloped in smoke. There was one about 10 yards from our house and the smoke was dreadful for my father who was, by then, very ill. He died ten days after D-Day. I remember feeling very proud when military policemen stood to attention as we followed my father's coffin.

The holiday camps in the area were taken over and it was mostly Canadian troops who came there to recuperate after being injured. They would get rounded up when the pubs closed and marched back to the camps. Living in the centre of town, we had a grandstand view of everything that went on. I remember seeing the military police trying to round up a group of tipsy soldiers, some with crutches, some with arms in slings, trailing back to camp and doing an impromptu dance at they were ushered along.

The feeling of exhilaration on VE-Day was something that you had to be there to appreciate. My family were teetotal, but there was a bottle of sherry in the sideboard that someone had given them. My mother was out and some friends and I decided that it would be a good idea to have a drink. We felt very naughty having a few sips each, but then wondered if my mother would look at the bottle and realise that some was missing. We hastily topped it up with water and knew that she would never taste it to find out what we'd done.

Robert Welham

Unlike many children at the outbreak of the war, sent off from home with a small suitcase and a nametag hung around their necks, I was not evacuated until late 1944, less than a year before the end of the war.

The reason for our departure, I believe, was the coming of the V1s, the 'doodlebugs'. My mother, at 5 foot 2 inches and 6 stone, was not, as you can imagine, a physically strong woman. Yet, with my father away in North Africa, her mother sick, and me a mere five years old, she had managed to hold out through the entire Blitz before events finally took their toll.

The exact date we left Leytonstone in East London, I am not sure of. It was only after some recent research that I think it must have been in the July. The first doodlebug had fallen on 13 June, seven days after my fifth birthday. My mother and I were out shopping when we heard the heart-quickening sound of the air-raid siren and raced for the nearest communal shelter, which luckily was just round the corner. We sat with others along a long bench in total silence, listening to the heavy rumble of the approaching V1. It must have been to our right but it sounded overhead. As its engine cut out we waited for the inevitable explosion, which came five seconds later, a few streets away.

Having researched the map showing where all bombs, shells, V1s, and V2s fell in my area at Vestry House Museum in Walthamstow, I found out why I only heard that one bomb. It had been the first to fall in our area on 5 July in Harrington Road. Although flying bombs were falling thick and fast, there was not another one nearby until the 27th. This one struck a bus and demolished a block of flats half a mile from our home, causing thirty-one deaths.

It was not long after this that we evacuated. No one is around anymore for me to ask who arranged the evacuation, but it was 'unofficial', as we made our own arrangements.... My mother, grandmother, and I joined my Aunt Eileen, her three-year-old son Eddie, and her mother in Brierley, barely a hamlet in the Forest of Dean.

Many of these memories rank among my first. I was used to town life, with plenty of shops within easy reach and lots of people. Suddenly I was in the country. Admittedly, at home there had been the Wanstead Flats, a wide expanse of open grassland bordered by some forest, but this was the Forest of Dean, a real forest.

We had travelled down by train, crowded with soldiers and sailors, standing all the way. No one gave my mother or me a seat. I don't even remember my grandmother being with us, but she must have been. On this journey we crossed the River Severn and saw far below several Sunderland Flying Boats moored close to the bridge, no doubt waiting to go out into the Atlantic to search for enemy U-Boats.

Brierley consisted of six semi-detached council houses plus a few detached private houses along one side of the main A4136 road, a planation opposite, and some bungalows around the corner in a short unmade side-road. This all became familiar to me in the following six months. A nearby road led to Ruedean, where the school was that I should have attended, but didn't. There was also a large greengrocers and a small post office where I would sit on the counter and play with the weights and scales while the grown-ups talked. Further along on the grass verge was a line of bombs stacked two high that I would dare Eddie to touch. They must have belonged to the nearby American airbase; we saw several US servicemen around who gave the local children badges and chewing gum.

We first lodged with a Miss Frost in one of the semi-detached council houses with cabbages growing in the front garden. Miss Frost was a sharp-faced, bespectacled woman of middle age—lacking any humour and, like her name, 'frosty by nature'. I had a teacher's blackboard pointer I found from somewhere (perhaps it was hers, as I believe she had been a teacher), which I used as my sword. One day, irritated by my antics, she snatched it from me and threw it on the fire. In hindsight, perhaps I am being a bit harsh; living alone in her own world she no doubt resented having to have strangers foisted upon her.

Next door lived a little girl about my own age, Kathleen. I hardly remember her but I recall she had an enormous doll's house, complete with furniture and miniature dinner service, of which my favourite piece was a tiny milk jug. There were also two brothers close by, perhaps in their early teens, who copied cartoons out of the newspapers in thick black India ink. Their other drawings were of coal-mining cages with the lifting gear wheels at the top which they used to bomb with blobs of black ink. They also made model aeroplanes from balsawood kits which hung from the ceiling.

We held out with 'frosty face' for three months before moving into a bungalow around the corner with Mrs Morgan. She was far more accommodating; her husband, like my father, was in the Army. In the back garden was a sty with two pigs which Eddie and I once fed with stinging nettles. Much to our surprise the pigs didn't seem to mind. They just gobbled them up. I was used to seeing cows on Wanstead Flats, but I had never seen pigs before or sheep that grazed in a nearby field or horsemen riding along the skyline. Mrs Morgan had two teenage children, Gordon and Jean, who would take me around with them exploring the countryside. I especially enjoyed the deep forests with tiny fast-running streams. They once excitedly pointed out a fox lower down in an old quarry, but I didn't see it. The area was still a coal-mining region and possessed a narrow gauge railway where a small one truck carrying coal would move slowly along the track until it bumped into another, stationary truck. The resulting bump sent the stationary truck off, leaving the moving truck in its place, awaiting the next gentle collision.

Gordon and Jean didn't seem to mix with the other local youths, who all seem to have been boys and older than me. They made catapults and built ridge tents out of cut branches and string, substituting fern leaves for canvas. They looked very snug, but as a stranger I was never allowed inside.

Occasionally we would go shopping in Cinderford or Coleford or to the cinema, where we must have seen a Fred Astaire and Ginger Rogers musical, as that night I dreamt of two tiny figures in evening dress dancing around the cabbages in the front garden. I have a lot of memories of this time, like hearing my mother and aunt discussing the new V2 rockets that, unlike the V1s, descended from a great height and exploded before anyone heard them coming. No one at the time knew anything about travelling faster than sound.

On a lighter note, there were smells, tastes, and sounds. Sweets were on ration and a luxury, like the delicious Turkish delight that my father had sent us. A sugary crystalline texture, far better than the rubbery jelly covered in icing sugar we get today. I can't remember Christmas that year, nor any presents, but with the coming of the New Year 1945 I remember the snow and a valuable lesson.

I had gone into the plantation that lay across the main road with Gordon and Jean, to where a crowd of local children were sliding and skating on a small frozen pond. One boy, taller than the rest, was gliding up and down clearing away the snow with a broom. Skating looked easy. Everyone was doing it. Standing next to me at the edge of the ice was a little girl, well wrapped up against the cold. Apart from Jean and Kathleen, she was the only other girl I remember in the whole six months. I decided to show her how skating should be done. Running forward I launched myself onto the ice. Whoosh! Thud! I was carried off having banged my head. I never found out what happened to the little girl or what she thought or where she went, but I doubt she was impressed.

With the coming of winter and local talk of Brierley being cut off, my mother decided it was time to return home. There was the other worry, always at the back of her mind, of someone taking over our house. With people being bombed out, taking possession of empty properties did take place. This happened to one of my relatives in reverse. They were bombed out and took over an empty house whose previous residents never returned. My relatives eventually purchased the property. True, out house was only rented, but there was all our furniture and belongings.

We returned home around February or March. The end of war in Europe ended on 8 May was followed by a victory street party marking VE-Day, with a second street party celebrating the victory over Japan in August. Sometime between these two dates I started school (a year late), and at last my father came home.

I made a day-trip to Brierley with my parents in 1979. Little had changed. Cabbages were still growing in Miss Frost's front garden, although Miss Frost was no longer with us, and Mrs Morgan had moved away. Standing outside her bungalow an elderly lady from next door came out and invited us in for tea and cake. Out of her front room window I saw several horsemen galloping across the skyline, just as they had thirty years before.

31

Margaret Newton (née Littler)

I was born on 16 July 1935 at Blithbury Road, Dagenham.

In September 1940 my brother and I were evacuated. I remember our mother telling us we were not to be separated and we were to stay together. I cannot remember the journey to Northampton, but my brother said we went by train. My earliest memory is arriving at this very dark school with lots of ladies with clip boards, trying to sort us out. I do remember telling them that my Mum said we are not to be separated.

This lady took us down a very dark street to 2 Red Row, Raunds. We were taken in and introduced to Grandma Bailey and her daughter, Auntie Vi. They were lovely people. Before we went to bed, Auntie Vi game us each a packet of Rowntree's fruit gums. To this day, they still remind me of Auntie Vi.

In the morning I was taken to the school where we had been the night before. It was still a dark and dreary place with old-fashioned desks and benches, together with splinters. I remember complaining that I had splinters in my knickers! I didn't take too kindly to this old school, so in the afternoon I took myself up to the new council school and said I was wanted to go to school there. As luck would have it, I was allowed to stay there. It came out later that the father of Grandma Bailey's son-in-law was on its Board of Governors. What a bit of luck!

The same gentleman, a Mr Camozzi, also owned the Carlton Cinema and the local General Stores, Palmers. They lived in the Manor House, a grand old house with large gardens. It had what were at one time stables which had been converted into two small rooms, where Grandma's daughter Aunt Eve taught the piano. I didn't get a chance to learn the piano, but I think I would have liked to have had the opportunity. Speaking of piano, an old gentleman lived next door to Grandma, and me being an 'into everything' child, I said I would play 'Roll out the Barrel' to him on the piano. The family never let me forget this.

Grandma had these fascinating candlesticks in her parlour. They were very large, made of china, and with the loveliest crystal drops. As a child I had never seen anything so beautiful. I wasn't allowed to touch them but given the chance, if nobody was about, I was drawn to them. Grandma also had a glass dome with some stuffed birds inside. Once again, I had never seen anything like it before and another thing Grandma didn't have any electricity, only gas, so you can imagine looking at the gas mantle. It drew me like a magnet. Each Friday Grandma would go up to get her pension, leaving my brother to look after me. Well, I took this opportunity to get a really close look at this gas mantle and of course touched and broke it. My brother got the blame for letting me do it, but me being such an inquisitive child he didn't have a chance—so sorry bruv for causing you grief.

Raunds was surrounded by boot factories. I think there were about six altogether. After the war I found out that the Spurs player Danny Blanchflower had his boots made at Coggins factory.

As I mentioned before, Mr Camozzi owned the Carlton Cinema, so each Saturday I would go with Grandma to the pictures but made a pest of myself after about ten minutes, so was taken out to the front office to wait for Grandma to see her film. It was the same each Saturday. We would come out and I was holding Grandma's hand. She had the torch and I would say, 'Let me hold the torch Grandma,' and she would say, 'No, you mustn't show the Germans the light.' 'I won't,' I would say. So in the end she would give me the torch, and I would straight away flash it in the air. 'You little bugger,' Grandma would say—but it happened each week. Poor old love, I loved her and Auntie Vi so much.

On Saturday afternoons, one member of the family would open up the Carlton and take bookings for the evening performances. I would go along with them, if for no other reason to give Grandma some peace. I would wander round the cinema all on my own, having a wonderful time making up games; it was lovely.

I suppose a five year old was too much for an elderly lady, so sadly, I was re-billeted to another couple in Raunds. He was the local blacksmith and used to let me ride the horses when taking them back to their owners. I only stayed there a short time and once again was re-billeted to another couple, Mr and Mrs Prentice. I stayed with them until the end of the war. My parents would come and visit as often as they could. For a while my mother was in hospital in Bedfordshire, whereupon my father would come down Friday night until Monday morning and we would go and visit her. The friendship between Mr and Mrs Prentice and my parents lasted until they all passed on. To this day I keep in touch with Mrs Prentice's daughter. She is now in her nineties and we speak on the phone every three weeks or so. When I married my husband Bill in September 1957, Auntie Vi and Mr and Mrs Prentice came to our wedding.

I would like to take this opportunity to thank the people of Raunds for their kindness; it must have been as much of a traumatic time for them having 'us London kids' as it was for us. My memories of the war are good, apart from being parted from my Mum and Dad. I was well looked after and didn't know what it was to go to bed hungry or dirty.

32

P. M. Irving

When the Second World War broke out I was living in France with my family in the seaside town of Dinard, Brittany. I attended a French school and only spoke English at home.

At first, nothing seemed to change. The French people could not face another war on their soil and made no effort towards any sort of war work—this was left to the girl guides and boy scouts who were rallied to help!

In May/June 1940 all the schools were closed to be made into Army barracks and the hotels were turned into hospitals. Refugees started arriving from the North East as the Germans advanced.

I was aged twelve and was kept very busy as a girl guide, helping to deliver milk, meeting trains to help with babies and children *etc.*, and serving meals to the refugees who were pouring into the town.

After Dunkirk the French gave up, so the Germans advanced rapidly through France with no opposition and took everybody by surprise. Friends of ours had two hours' notice to get out of Paris and drove straight to us. The following day my father consulted the British Consulate, who told us that the Germans were approaching Reims and advised us to leave the next day when a boat was being sent out from UK. We needed to be at St Malo at 7 a.m. on Saturday 10 June and there was only one more boat the following day.

My parents packed all night and we closed up the apartment and left at 6 a.m. by car. We met up with our friends from Paris and stood on the quay waiting for the boat. It eventually arrived about midday.

Also waiting were English soldiers and sailors and some wounded on stretchers. They boarded first and then English people were allowed to board, carrying their luggage. We were allocated a small four-berth cabin for my parents, me, and my brother who was sixteen, but we preferred to remain on deck. Our friends had two adult children, a daughter aged eleven, and two dogs. The boat, a small cross-Channel ferry; soon sailed out to sea and we could see land which we thought was Guernsey or Jersey, but to our dismay was the coast of France, probably Normandy. Owing to submarines nearby, the boat was directed to shallow waters.

Eventually, the all-clear came and we set off into the Channel again much to everybody's relief, until a German plane appeared overhead. Fortunately, having circled us it decided to leave us alone and disappeared. The soldiers had set up a machine gun and were aiming at the plane but the officer yelled at them not to shoot, which probably saved us. The boat had been to Dunkirk and was damaged and leaking and having to be constantly pumped out.

About 10 p.m. it was getting dark and we were told we were now in the English Channel and safe. So my mother, who during the night had made sandwiches, called us all down into the cabin and gave everybody a sandwich, the first food that day. We were just about to start when our friends came into the cabin to warn us we were going through a 'swept channel' and that there was a danger of loose mines. We all immediately returned on deck holding our sandwiches.

About midnight we landed at Southampton and were allowed to stay on board until 6 a.m. Sunday morning, when the boat had to return to France.

The dogs could not be landed due to quarantine laws, so remained on ship and made several journeys, eventually landing in Wales and after quarantine were returned to the family.

33

Lynn Merritt

I spent the war years living in the Lodge at Michaelstowe Hall in Ramsey, Essex, a mansion of red brick in Georgian style built in 1903, where my father was head gardener. We moved there in 1938 when I was four years old, to an idyllic, overgrown landscaped garden which originally supported sixty gardeners, now only three of them. It had been a convalescent home belonging to Essex County Council, but was requisitioned by the Admiralty in 1941 and became an officers' club, Harwich and Parkeston being an important port during the war.

I remember the building had sandbags all round it. The formal flower beds were replanted with carrots and beetroot, and the big lawn was ploughed up for potato growing.

I don't have many memories of the naval officers, but we were able to get to know some of the sailors from the ships down at Parkeston Quay.

The Lodge was about half an hour's walk from the quay and outside the gates were comfortable brick walls to rest on, the grand wrought-iron gates and fence having been removed for 'the war effort'. My mother would sometimes invite two or three sailors in for a cup of tea and we became friends with some of them. I can clearly remember being given a shoebox with a mix of chocolate bars in it, particularly Fry's Chocolate Cream. You will be aware that chocolate was a rare treat at the time!

Being close to the port brought quite a lot of attention from the Germans. There were MTBs and Catalina planes based at Harwich/Felixstowe at the mouth of the Stour Estuary, and the river gave the enemy planes a point of reference on the East Coast. There was an ack-ack battery a few hundred yards away from our house which would have overlooked the river, so it became very noisy if enemy planes were spotted. I remember the searchlights in the sky, and hearing shrapnel rattling down in the laurel bushes as we dashed down to the air-raid shelter in the middle of the night ... some of it collected up in the morning as souvenirs.

Our shelter was an old mushroom-house on the edge of the wood at the bottom of the garden. It had a turf roof (possibly strengthened?) three or four steps down which we'd stumble, to some bunks made on the shelving where mushrooms were grown in better times. I can smell it still! We later had an Anderson shelter in the living room (fortunately quite a big room), and there were also nights spent crouching in the space under the stairs.

My father was an ARP warden and when the air-raid sirens sounded he had to bike about half a mile to his 'station' in some garages behind a pub in Dovercourt.

I was lucky enough not to be evacuated, as children near the coast mostly were. The boundary stopped at the end of our wood, 100 yards away, so I went to the village school in Ramsey. They had a long semi-underground shelter on the meadow at the back where we sat and sang songs (and probably also recited the multiplication tables), and everyone cheerfully accepted the conditions of damp and darkness. I can't remember what sort of lighting we had, but there must have been something.

I walked nearly a mile to school, sometimes spending a bit of pocket money on a hot roll straight from the oven at the bakery in the village. On the way home I could possibly treat myself to some ice-cream wafers at the village shop. There were alternatives to the lack of sweets!

I kept in touch with one of my teachers until she died in 2012 aged one-hundred-and-four. She was a friend of my mother who, also being a teacher, did supply teaching during the war. All through one very cold winter she cycled to a school in Mistley, about 5 or 6 miles each way. A kind family living opposite took me into their warm kitchen while I waited to be taken to school by their daughter, a few years older than me. I remember chilblains and damp mittens from those walks to school.

At the end of the war the Hall became an Army officers' club. A transit camp had to be built to house returning soldiers before they were demobbed, and several acres were requisitioned close by. Overseen by the British Army a large number of German POWs were housed in Warner's Holiday Camp, and as I cycled to and from the High School I often saw them marching up to the fields near my home. They were building substantial Army huts for several weeks. Some POWs were employed at the club, including Hans, an excellent mechanic, who helped to keep my father's car on the road, and kitchen staff, one of whom made me an amazing birthday cake, the best I had ever seen in my whole life.

At some stage in the war I remember going to ENSA concerts down on the quay, so obviously local people were in invited to go, though I imagine this wouldn't have been at the height of the war. I fell for a fair-haired drummer in the band.

I can actually remember 'The Day War Broke Out'. Somehow this is embedded in my memory. My parents decided that we would cycle down to the sea at Earlhams Beach, near Dovercourt as it was such a beautiful day. From Ramsey there were paths along the top of the dykes among the marshes. I was sitting in a child's seat on the back of my father's bike and I must have sensed that this could be the last time we'd ever be free to make this trip. I do remember that there were soon all kinds of tank-traps and barbed wire on the beaches.

From a very early age I kept rabbits, which were not looked upon as pets but for the pot. I soon branched out into keeping chickens. I supplied one of our gardeners and us three with eggs and had to have some part of each one's ration book to get a supply of meal. I cooked up potato peelings and all kinds of waste food on a Primus stove in the potting shed, and weeded the garden of nutritious green stuff for my chickens. In the autumn I kept the cockerel in a smaller run to fatten him up for Christmas. My father had snares hanging in the shed to add to our own home-bred rabbits. I also grew a few vegetables in my own plot in the garden, and consequently turned to a career in horticulture when I grew up.

My mother never failed to remind me over the years that I had a keen sense of business, if a little underhand. I sold eggs to the gardener and to my mother, who also paid the food bills.

I have enjoyed this trip back to my childhood ... a very happy one despite the war.

34

Angela Aston

Three o'clock; a whole hour had gone past since I was woken up by an unfamiliar sound. My father called it an air-raid warning. The air-raid—whatever that was—didn't make as much noise as the warning. In fact there had been no sound at all since the siren warned us. We seemed to be the only people awake.

Sleepily, mother read the instruction card issued to every household. 'Come on, back to bed,' she yawned. 'We must have slept through the warning. That was the all-clear.' So ended my first encounter with the war. I had enjoyed every minute of that hour. To a child of five, what could be more exciting than getting up at a forbidden hour and sitting in a deck-chair in the pantry?

My parents didn't share my enthusiasm. Father, six feet tall, had to duck beneath shelves, and mother's legs became entangled with vegetables as she wearily groped for the doorknob. It was the first of many such nights.

My friends and I were old enough to find all the changes exciting without realising the horror of war. We had a status symbol too—our blue ration books. Not for us, the green books of babies and toddlers. Now everyone knew we went to school. Going to school became an adventure. At all times we had to carry our identity discs and gas masks. Sometimes the warning would sound while we were walking home from school. Then we would run to the nearest shelter. No-one minded, even if they didn't know us.

At school our shelter was a musty, damp cellar, with benches placed against newly distempered walls. Another lesson was added to the time-table—that of 'Let's pretend there's an air-raid.' A mass of giggly children made their way to the hitherto unknown cellar, then teachers ordered, 'gas masks on.' This was the signal for mass hysteria. Imagine several dozen heads, each looking like something from outer space with voices to match, and you will see why we thought it was so funny.

It was a great day when our friends next door got an Anderson shelter in their garden. We were to share it, so while the adults tried to make it comfortable with rugs for the floor and blankets on the bunks, I was sorting through more interesting things. I had to decide which books and games should be kept there.

Suddenly I noticed my father pulling the fence down. Whatever was he doing? Mother explained that if we were to reach the shelter quickly we would have to make a path through the gardens.

As she spoke I realised that there were other advantages too. Now I would be able to go round to Auntie's other times as well. She was always willing to sit telling stories to me. Wartime was becoming fun. That night I was so excited I couldn't sleep. I wondered what it would be like to lie on a bunk and made up my mind to be first into the shelter, so that I could get onto the top one. At last I fell asleep and only woke up when mother called me to get up or I would be late for school. 'Jerry' hadn't been that night; what a disappointment; what a waste. Mother assured me he would be back.

Sure enough, the following night I woke up to the familiar wail of the siren. Remembering where we had to go, I was soon dressed. Moonlight gave the trees an eerie look. All around us, disembodied voices could be heard as everyone scurried to safety. Occasionally an air-raid warden shouted, 'Put that light out,' or 'Close those curtains properly.' I was glad to reach the shelter. My father and the other men stayed outside in case they were needed to man the stirrup pumps. When we were inside the fun really began. Mother and Auntie unpacked food and opened thermos flasks. Were those really the sandwiches I disliked at teatime? They tasted good now.

We soon learned to recognise our own planes. Their engines sounded much smoother than those of the Germans. Theirs chugged, sounding so heavy that it often seemed as if they, as well as their bombs, would fall from the sky. With an ack-ack gun stationed on a nearby farm and searchlights all around, at least they didn't hang about. Barrage balloons became a familiar sight. They seemed to interest adults as much as children. Whenever one was sent up or pulled down, a face turned skyward was enough to attract attention all round.

Tuesday nights were special, although I doubt if that was what my parents called them. Tuesday nights were one long cuddle, as I slept with my mother while my father was fire-watching at his office. Only once can I remember being afraid on a Tuesday night. The sky in the direction of father's office was a deep pink after an air-raid. Mother told me that it meant a lot of bombs had been dropped in that area. As soon as the air-raid was over, she went to the telephone kiosk on the corner, but the line was dead. We didn't go back to bed that night. It was many hours before he got a message to us. That night I glimpsed the reason why grown-ups didn't see war as an adventure.

Because we lived on the outskirts of a large city, we would wake up to find buses parked nearby—in the roads, the park, or the fields beyond. They were brought from the inner city garages, as these were targets for the bombers. Suddenly the quiet suburban road that was home became a hive of activity in the early mornings.

Children who were evacuated may have been safer and have memories of country life, but we who stayed behind lived through a drama that those too young to understand danger will remember as an adventure equal to any in children's' fiction books.

I lived in Birmingham during the war with my mother and father, who had served in the First World War and was over forty, so was not called up. A conscientious objector lived nearby and I remember him being rather aloof, but maybe that was because people talked about 'conchies' in a disparaging way. Arthur, who lived next door, was a teenager who hoped to get into the Fleet Air Arm, but was turned down because of flat feet. Instead he was sent as a Bevin Boy to a coalfield in Nottinghamshire. His widowed mother then had a teacher billeted with her. She had come to teach in a school where the male teachers had been called up. I liked her and wished my own teachers were as nice. Because Arthur worked in mines they had a lot more coal delivered than the rest of us—more than they could possibly use, so we had half of it most times.

We went on holiday to Devon the day before war broke out. We had to change trains several times and were shunted off into sidings at least once due to troops on the move. Some walked along on the outside of the carriages risking their lives, perhaps because they knew they may not return anyway and were showing bravado.

My mother made me a siren suit out of pink cot blankets. It was lovely and warm, laid on the bottom of my bed ready to put on as soon as the siren wailed. My parents had moved my bed into their bedroom, as mother was worried in case my room was cut off from theirs in the event of a bomb dropping on our house. We were lucky. Only on one night incendiary bombs landed in our road. Several bombs fell in gardens and one unlucky family had one through the roof. Later in the war we were issued with our own Morrison shelter. The dining table was put in another room and the rest of the furniture squashed up to make room. I liked having it as I used it as a stage to dance on. I was sad to see it go at the end of the war!

Like all housewives, my mother became adept at managing to make meals out of whatever was to hand. She had a recipe to make sponge cake with liquid paraffin instead of fat. It doesn't sound appetising but was very light, and she was paid many compliments about it. She was also good at needlework and knitting, and always managed to make my dresses even if it meant using various bits and pieces. I had a navy winter school coat and when I grew out of it, she cut it in two places, sewed in some dark material, and covered it with navy ribbon. My form teacher told me off, saying that it wasn't uniform, but when I told her it was my old coat, she was very impressed with my mother's handiwork.

The photos were taken by my mother on that holiday at the beginning of the war. I was sitting with my father in a park at Paignton.

35

Ivor Peters

Even at the age of eighty-two, I can still remember all those years ago as a young village boy of Gunnislake in Cornwall, when we heard that children would be coming to the village as evacuees.

I was about nine or ten when the village women said we would be having children come from cities like London or Plymouth. On the day some of them arrived at our railway station, there were officials waiting with women who were to take them in. We saw children of different ages; some had been sick on their journey, some had messed themselves, and some were in a pitiful state from travelling.

We local boys sat on the railway railings and watched them being taken away to their temporary homes. After being registered in by officials we heard that they would be going to school with us eventually. Some of the older boy evacuees looked at us locals with a bit of hatred and were spoiling for a fight to show their toughness and cocky attitude—when they arrived, that is.

Those who came to our school were placed in various classes at the start and on their first day at playtime the evacuee boys decided to have a go at us local boys (but underestimated us). Many of them had a few black eyes and loose teeth by the time the whistle went for us to go into class. We locals also had a few loose teeth as well! The teachers laid down *strict* rules after that incident, but somehow we became good friends with them after a couple of days. The ladies who they were billeted with did not let them out much at first as they wanted to keep them safe and looked after. After a while, we asked the ladies if they could come out with us local lads to play, which they did. We taught them how to climb trees, to swim in the River Tamar, and anything else we did ourselves, such as Tarzan swinging out into the river and letting go. The things we taught them back in those days were dangerous, but we saw no fear.

As they settled in, evacuees and locals helped out on farms and market gardens. Also, 'dig for victory' had started when every piece of ground had to be used to grow anything for the war effort. Some farmers would pay us for working for them, but there were others who thought it was good cheap labour.

Those who didn't pay much for working for them would have things stolen from their fields. It was also surprising that the evacuees started to look healthier in their colour by living in the countryside, not as white as when they first arrived.

Food was very scarce at the time and neighbours would share food with one another to help feed us.

Most children had free dinners at school and the schools used to try and grow vegetables as well on any spare ground. Some evacuees used to tell us that their stomachs used to rattle because they were hungry and we locals used to tell them to fill up by drinking lots of water.

Some evacuees were sent back to where they came from for all sorts of reasons and when some evacuee children's parents arrived to see their children, some children didn't recognise their own parents and would hide away.

The freedom that we had in those hard days of the war was beneficial, enabling us to get outdoors and try and work for food on farms. Harvest time was always fun in the summer when we used to assist with gathering in the wheat or hay as we were given a pasty by the farmer's wife. This would be meat and potato, cheese, corned beef, or something sweeter, such as a cherry or raspberry pasty. It would then be followed by milk from the farm for us young ones and the adults would have cider out in the fields. Many a time we would sneak a drink from the cider barrel, which would make us a bit tipsy.

Life was very hard back in those days until the Americans came to England, some of whom were stationed in our village. We would ask them for 'gum' or sweets, which they always had, and sometimes we were given a tin of spam for our mothers. Somehow the village altered from the time the Americans came, as it took us away from working on the farms and what we had achieved by working so hard. The Americans and English and other troops who lived beside the hedgerows for weeks disappeared overnight. We heard that they had all been sent to sea ports along the coast. A few days later it was announced that D-Day had come, and all those men had gone over for the occasion. The village became so quiet after the troops had departed, and we then returned to the farms to help again until the end of the war.

I have often wondered over the years where most of the evacuees were who had stayed with us all those years ago and what happened to them. I also think about the poor but happy times we had. They were happy memories.

36

Derrick Finch

I lived with my parents, my brother who was six years older than me, and my sister who was six years younger in Manor Park. Our house had two bedrooms, no bathroom, no hot water and an outside toilet. My Dad worked in London as a gatekeeper when they were re-building the Bank of England.

Before the First World War he had worked as a compositor in one of the London newspaper offices; but he was gassed and was unable to continue his trade as his lungs were badly damaged. Therefore, he wasn't called up to serve in the Second World War, but spent time in the civil defence.

I remember the months leading up to the war and hopes that there would not be one. We had to register to get identity cards and ration books. I remember queuing to collect our gas masks. My sister had a Minnie Mouse one which was red with a nose piece that flapped as she breathed. Wearing them was stifling. We had an Anderson air-raid shelter for which a hole had to be dug about 4 feet deep, then earth had to be piled on top. Ours wasn't very good as we had to keep bailing it out. Eventually it was replaced with a brick-built one. I lost a lot of schooling as they were building air-raid shelters in the playground. The railings outside our house were taken away for use in the war effort.

Quite soon after war was declared my brother was evacuated to Swindon with his whole school, East Ham Grammar. He later joined the air force and served in India. My mother, sister, and I, as well as two children from next door, were evacuated to Southwold, but we did not stay there very long.

As the war progressed we had to black out our windows. Woes betide anyone who dared to let a tiny light escape. Then in 1940 an official letter was sent to my Mum and Dad telling them that they wanted to take as many children away as possible for safety. Mum and Dad did much soul-searching as to whether to send me. I was a very nervous child and had never been away from my parents. However, the daughter of a friend, Peggy, who was nine-and-a-half, one year older than me and much more self-sufficient, was going, so my name was included, but on the proviso that we were not to be separated.

So on 17 June 1940, three double-decker buses set out from Cornwell School, Walton Road, to Paddington, and we off for who-knew-where.

We eventually arrived at our destination, Pentewan, approximately forty children and Miss Brown our teacher. Being chosen was a traumatic experience, especially as

I *was* separated from Peggy. However, she was billeted next door to me. We could not have been treated better. Such love was shown to us from these Christian people. Peggy's billet was with Auntie Edna and Uncle Jack James. Auntie Etta and Uncle Charlie Couch who was the billeting officer took me in.

His mother, Mrs Couch (Gran) lived in a house up some steps next to the church with her daughter, Auntie Hannah, and her husband, Uncle Fred Tremberth. We were made to feel very much at home at 'Hillside'. Indeed I was to spend many hours in the garage of that house making toys out of driftwood. It was quite dark when we walked across the village to our billets. Tymor, Uncle Charlie's house, had a figurehead of a ship in the garden. He was a shipbroker. They had no children and wanted to adopt me at the end of the war.

The house next door was connected by a pathway at the back. I was assured that Peggy wasn't far away and would see me in the morning, and as the magic of living in such a beautiful village began, the memory and love of the place and people will never leave me.

After a while, the village school that had been closed for years was opened up for us. Very soon it became needed as an Army barracks. We were without school for well over a year. Eventually we were given a Sunday school hall and Miss Brown had to cope with approximately fifty children of mixed ages. I remained there until I was eleven and then I went to Mevagissey School.

American soldiers were stationed nearby, and on the beach near to the village they would bring landing craft up onto the sand. They would allow us to go on these. If we saw them we would ask, 'Got any gum chum?' It usually had the desired effect. Sometimes they would give us a tin of coffee as well, and one boy was even lucky enough to be given a bicycle.

My parents visited me and also paid my fare to go home for fortnight holidays in spite of the air-raids. I saw a V1 flying bomb go over my house just as the motor switched off. It carried on flying and blew up further down our street. One time I went to a pantomime in the Ilford Hippodrome, and three days later a V2 landed on some houses behind it. Many were killed. None were killed in the Hippodrome, but I don't know if any were injured. The blast shook our house about ½ mile away. While I was in London one summer, Pentewan was bombed. No one was badly hurt or killed. A huge piece of shrapnel had landed where I usually worked. Had I been there I would have been killed, but I was due back to Cornwall the following day.

My mother and sister were privately evacuated to Biscovey but had a bad billet. Eventually they came to Pentewan for a few months, returning home to try to tidy our house which was damaged by a mine dropped further down the road.

If there was ever an air-raid, Uncle Charlie would receive a telephone call. He would then pass the information onto Mr Billing and whistles would be blown. When the all-clear call came, a hand bell would let everyone know. When Plymouth was bombed it continued night after night.

There were lots of things for us evacuees to do that we wouldn't have experienced in London. We would visit the blacksmiths to watch the horses being shoed, never understanding how the hot shoes didn't hurt the horses. There was a large farm nearby that allowed us to pick the windfall apples and we were allowed to eat as many as we wished. We were soon tired of eating them as you may guess. I went blackberry-picking and enjoyed them stewed and in pies.

I remained in Pentewan till after VE-Day and I was there for five years. When the war in Europe was over the whole village had a street party decked with flags.

I found returning home rather strange, having to get used to living in London after being in a beautiful village. Most of the houses in my road were damaged.

The rationing continued long after the war and we had to queue for everything. I remember queuing at Mills the Bakers for a loaf of bread costing 4½*d*; eggs were rationed and sometimes we used dried egg, which I found most enjoyable. Also toast and beef dripping—very tasty.

I spent just six months in school and left at the age of fourteen. I tried to catch up on my education by attending evening classes.

I will never forget the happy years I spent there and the love shown to us.

37

Donald Jackson

I suppose I was only a true vaccie for about a week.

I was born in December 1931 and was nearly eight on 1 September 1939. The first I knew of the war was being woken early and taken to Halbutt Street Senior School with my Mum and six-month-old brother. I can't remember if my fourteen-to-fifteen-year-old brother came. We were taken by motor coach to the Princess Cinema, New Road, Dagenham, and then walked down Kent Avenue on the Fords Estate. We were six or eight deep on the pavement and that was the longest walk I have ever made. My Mum was carrying my kid brother and all our belongings including the large baby gas mask.

When we reached the Ford Motor Company jetty, there were seven paddle steamers berthed. We boarded one of the three destined for Felixstowe. The *Crested Eagle*, *Medway Queen*, and *Thames Queen* were going to Felixstowe; the *Royal Eagle* and *Royal Daffodil* off to Lowestoft; and the *Golden Eagle* and *Queen of the Channel* to Great Yarmouth. I believe only the *Medway Queen* survived the war; some were lost at Dunkirk, and she is now a wreck. Off we sailed; I can't remember seeing another one of the boats *en route*.

When we were the furthest from the coast, someone said they saw a periscope and a naval destroyer (come to our rescue?). All knowledge of this event has been denied by the Admiralty, I've been told. But we know what we saw. A call went out on the boat's tannoy for people to move away from the starboard side because there was a chance the boat would turn turtle.

We docked at Felixstowe Pier and stayed the night in an empty hotel on the seafront. We were bedded down on about 9 inches of straw which some would find hard to believe. Next day we were taken by coach to Woodbridge and were billeted in an old house that was furnished (as such) and had been empty for many years after the owner had died. This was in a long terrace of houses. It was very dirty, dusty, and musty. My Dad visited us the following weekend and because nothing was happening during the Phoney War period, he brought us home to Dagenham.

On 1 September 1939 nearly 17,000 were evacuated from Fords Jetty. On 2 September the same boats serviced Gravesend, Kent.

I remember the Anderson shelter being delivered (more like thrown in the front garden). My cousin Fred Jackson from Heathway helped my Dad to install it; it was very elaborate, with a sealed door in case of a gas raid. It had a large porch and another sealed door. Fred told my Dad to wait for him to come home after the war (we were never going to lose the war) to help him remove the shelter. He was a corporal in the REME and sadly he was killed at Monte Cassino.

My kid brother had one of the large baby gas things—hardly a mask—which we had to manually pump; fortunately, it was never used in anger. When the raids started at weekends my Dad was home. I used to get out of the shelter and stand behind him watching the action. All the men of the family stood outside the shelter entrance during a raid, no helmets or other protection either. I was so quiet he did not know I was behind him, but I was soon ordered back when he realised I was there. When my Dad and elder brother were at work, I was able to take charge and be gaffer. I think my Mum gave up with me. A cuff on the ear plus a lecture followed when Dad came home.

I think it was the first big raid on London that I recall. I watched the bombers. They seemed no more than rooftop high, wave after wave, the pilots and nose-gunner clearly visible. This then became the norm.

The Meloqs would come in first, shooting down barrage balloons in flames. The sky was full of 'Spits and Hurries' in dog fights. There were five ack-ack guns in Barking Park, four in Whalebone Lane, North Dagenham, and Parsloes Park in Dagenham held a battery of rockets. There was also a mobile AA gun on a lorry. All the windows in the houses along the south side of Longbridge Road, Barking, opposite the park, were boarded up. As soon as the all-clear went, all the kids searched the roads for shrapnel—sometimes very hot stuff. I think shrapnel did more damage than the bombs.

During one raid, a Saturday I think, a pilot was descending by parachute and the newly supplied rifles to the newly formed Home Guard were firing at him. My Dad was shouting out to stop shooting, but to no avail. The tale was that he was a Polish Spitfire pilot and he landed in the garage/petrol station in Wood Lane, Dagenham, next to the Merry Fiddlers pub. He had been wounded.

Our house was damaged by the bomb that fell in Maxey Road, and the bombing was getting worse. My parents decided that we should move to Oxfordshire. My Mum's sister and her family had already moved there from Dagenham. She managed to settle in with an old boy in Fulbrook, near Burford. He had been a widower for years and had three sons. One worked on a farm, lived in Fulbrook, and never liked us; one was in the RAMC; and the third was in the RAF. The second and third came home on leave and seemed to appreciate the better life and grub their father was getting for us being there. Sadly, Albert (the third son) was killed on the Burma railways, thanks to the Japs' brutality.

The factory in Hackney where my Dad worked was bombed and he was out of work. He cycled down to Fulbrook a couple of times, 100 miles each way, and decided to move with my elder brother from Dagenham to live with us. He worked on the Little Risington Bomberdrome. My brother worked in the Burford laundry until his enlistment in the RASC. I went to Burford School—not a happy three or four years. I loved the country and did not want to return to Dagenham in 1945.

The nearest I got to a bombing was when one fell in Swinbrook (the next village), killing a cow. You may have heard of Unity Mitford, an ardent admirer of Hitler's. She lived in that village and I often saw her. She was always on the bridge over the lovely Windrush River by the Swan pub. She used to cover her face with what I thought was flour, probably face powder. She is buried in the local churchyard.

When the war started I was attending Wood Lane School and shelters were built in the playgrounds. One week we would attend a shelter in the morning. The next week, the same shelter in the afternoon. Not too much was learnt, I assure you. Burford School was not much better for education. When we returned in 1945 I went to Halbert Street School for Boys. I seem to remember I got the cane for showing the workings of mental arithmetic. The Welsh bully of a teacher thought I was taking the mick. I had never been taught mental arithmetic. I left school on 18 December 1945 and started work on 20 December. The 22nd was my fourteenth birthday. I suppose on reflection I enjoyed the war, but I would not have said that if I had been a parent.

38

Stan Delves

In accordance with the Government evacuation scheme, in 1940 my brothers Jack (thirteen) and David (eight) and I (nine) assembled at our respective schools and walked to Dovercourt Station on the morning of the 2 June.

Jack went on the 0907 train to Kington in Herefordshire, David and I on the earlier train at 0817 to Thornbury, Gloucestershire. The 0817 direct train stopped at Ipswich, Cambridge, Bedford, Yate, and arrived at Thornbury at tea time that day.

The packed food and drink soon went on the journey, and a hungry pair of brothers joined others assembled outside Thornbury Station full of adventure. Transport took David and me to Berkeley School playground, where our respective foster parents were waiting.

We had been allocated to a Mr and Mrs Love and went with them to their house situated outside the castle. Mr Love was employed by the dowager countess of Berkeley; she always dressed in black, and took an interest in evacuees when they arrived. We played in the castle grounds chasing the peacocks, swimming in her pool, and generally having the freedom of the place. Local children took umbrage at the attention we evacuees got from her and fights sometimes broke out.

All went well until my brother David, always on a short fuse, threw a plate at Mr Love after being corrected over something. The result was that David was transferred to the malt house at Morton under the care of district nurse Nora Corran, and I to new foster parents, Mr and Mrs Cole, at Berkeley Heath a mile or so away.

The three brothers were now completely separated. Jack at Leominster, David at Morton, and I at Berkeley Heath. Life was good at Berkeley Heath. Chickens and goats in the garden and the Cole's son, aged seven, to play with. Complete adventure, unlike urban Dovercourt. However, change was on the way. David was pining for his older brother (me), and I was taken by car to the malt house at Morton to join him. It was great to be re-united with him again, together with boys and girls from our hometown in Essex. Life was full of adventure at Morton. We attended Thornbury School on Wednesdays and church at Thornbury on Sundays. During playtime at Thornbury I used to play hiding under logs in the timber yard near the school, dangerous but daring.

We were encouraged to grow vegetables at Thornbury School in allotments which also served as air-raid shelters when the sirens went off. I can vividly remember the headmaster Mr Nichols coming to our classroom, distressed to tell us that the HMS *Hood* had been sunk, and joyously coming back a day or two later to say, 'we have sunk the *Bismark*.'

On the way back to Morton, we passed the home-bound team of horses pulling heavy logs to Thornbury Mill. The road was narrow and I was scared of the horses passing.
As the expected invasion of the east coast never happened, Mum and my Aunty came and fetched David and I home. We took a coach from Thornbury to Bristol during an air-raid, Bristol to Paddington by train across London in another Blitz, then Liverpool Street Station to Dovercourt to meet a hugging Dad. Jack came home a year later from Ludlow, Shropshire, a grown man.

Happy memories of Thornbury will never fade.

39

Celia Fawcett

Until 1935, when I was three years old, home to me was in the Galleons Reach stretch of the Thames, many years before development began. We lived in a row of cottages owned by the sewerage works where my father worked. The superintendent's house stood in its own grounds, while the key workers and their families lived in the cottages. Galleons Cottages, as they were named, were demolished *c.* 1935 when the company needed the ground to extend the plant.

In those days we were surrounded by fields and chickens were allowed to roam freely. It was great sport to hunt for eggs and I can remember the pleasure of finding a warm, newly laid egg among the weeds.

My elder sister was collected by the school bus as the cottages were quite isolated. When I was four years old we moved to the outskirts of Barking. Best for me were the marshes, just at the end of the road and across the A13. We used to cross the main road unsupervised, but nowadays it's a hazardous and almost impossible business with the juggernauts hurtling along.

Off we'd trot with an empty jam jar sporting a string round its neck, and our fishing nets. We spent hours and hours fishing for tiddlers in the streams that criss-cross the marshes, or trying to catch dragonflies as they darted through the reeds. Many a hapless frog leapt in terror when disturbed in the mud. We picked bunches of buttercups and hunted for wild violets, only returning home when we were hungry.

The A13 is lined with factories now and that particular part of marshland has been built on. I can't help but feel sad for the children brought up in the area now, who know no better than to watch TV or use their play stations. We had a field at the end of the garden where we'd play cricket and football, and our parents never had to fear for our safety. Sadly, a concrete jungle, complete with troubled families, has now replaced the field.

There was never a question of our staying away from school for no reason; indeed school was a place we looked forward to going. We did our drill, received toffees for good work, and learned the three 'r's without constant changes to the curriculum.

All this changed with the advent of the Second World War, when I was seven years old.

It is only in the past ten years or so that I've ceased having dreams of being machine-gunned. I can easily recall the dreaded rat-a-tat-tat as a lone fighter plane swooped down, directing its guns at the little terraced houses in Bath where my sisters and I had been evacuated.

At the beginning of the war, the decision was made to take all London's schoolchildren to places of safety. The allotted place for our school in Barking was Bath. I remember holding my elder sister's hand as we trotted to the coaches waiting to take us to Paddington Station. We were each given a gas mask, which was slung round our necks on a string, an orange, and a tube of Rowntree's clear gums. We were made to try the gas masks on but ripped them off to rid ourselves of the suffocating smell of rubber. I cried when I was put on the coach but was assured by my mother that it was only a rehearsal and we'd return home the next day.

When we reached our destination we were taken to some sort of clearing house and waited to be collected by our designated 'aunties and uncles'. Overhearing the grown-up conversations, I had by now realised that I was to stay for some time and proceeded to blub. Our stay was to last for three long years. In our new auntie's back yard she held me in her arms while conversing with her neighbours. 'Poor little thing, she's from the slums you know, I'll have to fatten her up.' What a good job our mother couldn't hear her; we'd moved into a brand new house with all 'mod cons' just three years previously....

My memories of staying in that house aren't good. My elder sister, who was eleven and four years older than me, did most of Auntie's house work, which included changing the bed I wet most nights. 'Auntie' and 'Uncle' had one daughter, Lorna, who was a week younger than me, and I hated her. She used to pull my hair when nobody was looking and when I shrieked I got into trouble. When my birthday and Christmas presents arrived from London, I had to share them with her. I well remember two beautiful new nightdresses arriving: one was blue, the other green. I was told by Auntie that I had to give one to her daughter as it wasn't fair that she should be left out. As I lived in her house, the daughter got first choice of colour.

We had to go to church three times on Sunday and more trouble was caused when I was chosen for the church choir and invited to perform solo for the Christmas service. Several mothers complained it wasn't fair for an evacuee to be selected over local children.

The nastiest thing Auntie and Uncle did was to allow their daughter to have cocoa and biscuits with her father when he returned home from work each evening, while my sister and I had to stay in the back garden in the chill autumn dusk. One weekend when my mother visited unexpectedly and when we told her of our treatment, she found us another family to stay with immediately.

The next family was wonderful, mainly because they didn't worry about cleanliness. There never seemed to be any hot water so they didn't insist we washed. We were joined there by our youngest sister, who had been too young to come with us at the beginning of the war. There was an old grandmother and about three daughters, one of whom went out with Yanks and brought home all sorts of treats. Another seemed to be perpetually pregnant and it was her job to look after us.

One of my duties was to go to visit one of the large hotels in the Landsdowne area and go down the steps into the kitchen. I used to say, 'Mrs Hallaway says I've come for

Danny's bones.' Danny was their wonderful, slobbery, dirty old dog. The chef would solemnly make me up a big bag of cooked meat bones and say how he hoped Danny would enjoy them. I suspect that chef was a friend of the daughter who 'went with Yanks'. When I arrived home we would all gnaw at the luscious meat while poor old Danny had to wait for the nearly bare pickings.

Then one night carnage erupted. Bath boasted one barrage balloon as its defence system, so when the Germans made a surprise reprisal attack, the city was a sitting duck.

We were shoved under Granny's bed (Granny's room was over the cellar!) when the sirens sounded and we remained there for the rest of the night while bomb after bomb exploded. The floors shook, ceilings came down, windows fell in, but worst of all was the rat-a-tat-tat of the machine guns from low-flying aircraft.

The next morning brought silence followed by our stunned parents later in the day, having heard the news on the radio. Our adoptive family kindly put them up for the night as all train services had been disrupted and they couldn't return home.

Gerry returned for a second time that night and our parents decided we would be as well to take our chances in London, if this was what could happen when we were supposed to be safely evacuated.

During the ensuing evenings back at our 'slum' my mother spent hours picking what we were told was glass from our hair. I found out years later that we were running alive with lice. I think the most distressing thing for her was that we returned speaking like country yokels. The neighbours would crowd around to hear us talk.

'Where be to?' 'Where'st bin?' we'd say, and then proceed to chatter in dialect just to annoy everybody.

During my stay I learned to enjoy the wonderful countryside and the plants and flowers I grew to love. I can still recollect the pungent smell of cowslips, although it's years since I've seen one. However, the strongest memory is of the machine gun which somehow seemed as though it was after me, personally.

On return from evacuation my small world had changed, but the memory of those earlier years lives on.

John Huke

I was a pupil at the Colchester Royal Grammar School during the Second World War. At the sounding of the air-raid warning in 1942 (I was eleven years old), we would all walk from our class rooms to the shelters situated across a tarmac playground, adjacent to Creffield Road. I have such a vivid memory of a crowd of us crossing the playground when a German single-seat fighter flew very low over our heads making an unusually raucous noise, we could clearly see the pilot's face. When we were all gathered in the shelter, the teacher told us that the plane had been machine-gunning us. Our reaction was one of excitement, no sense at all of the gravity of the occasion. We longed for the 'all-clear' so that we might search for bullets. There were none to be found, only rows of pock marks about a half inch deep in the tarmac. None of us were hit.

The event was soon put into the background; I don't think that I even bothered to tell my parents about it. We were probably quite naive, not as understanding of the world as children of today. In fact, the death of friends was a common happening, I remember one lad who sat at the front of the class was drowned one weekend in the sea at Walton; he had walked round the end of a groin into deep water. The class's reaction was, 'oh blow ... who will have to move into the front seat?' Others died of a variety of accidents and diseases.

George Osborn

Although I have written my own evacuee story in full, dedicated to my sister Brenda, I have set out below some excerpts to give a varied account of my time as an evacuee.

I wasn't very old on 3 September 1939. Five years and three months to be exact. I suppose the start of a World War and the events leading up to it must have been at least in the 'sensational' category to a small boy, because I do remember that first day of the war. It was, in fact, two days after my sister and I were evacuated, together with several thousands of other children from Portsmouth to the Isle of Wight. My sister Brenda was fifteen months older than me and I resented this. I was always trying to catch her up but never seemed to be able to. As soon as I was almost there, three when she was four, then four when she was five, she had another birthday and was two years older than me again; it just wasn't fair.

So with the onset of the Second World War we had been issued with gas masks which we had to carry in a strong cardboard box provided with a cord to sling over the shoulder. Younger children were offered a Mickey Mouse model. I had been offered one of these but would have rather been gassed than be seen in one. We regularly practised putting them on and off at school.

On our arrival at Ryde Pier on 1 September, Brenda and I were no more than 6 miles from our home in Portsmouth, but to us it might as well have been 100 miles. Most children over a certain age had been given a stamped addressed envelope to send back to their parents when they knew what their address would be. I didn't get one so it was assumed that my sister's card would suffice for the both of us. Our school had been kept together so we were all transported to the same area. The Infants School ended up in the village of Wootton, midway between Ryde and Newport.

After being paraded round like cattle at an auction in front of would-be foster parents who seemed reluctant to take on strange-speaking, unkempt evacuees from over the water, my sister was chosen by Mrs Gallop. Unfortunately she didn't want to take me, despite it being suggested that I would be happier staying with my sister. I was marched round the village with the other leftovers. We had been given a paper carrier bag containing a tin of condensed milk, another two tins (the contents of which I can't recall), and a very welcome bar of chocolate. We were tired and our small suitcases and bags, together with our gas masks hanging like lead around our shoulders, were making things worse. Brenda had walked part of the way with me until she had reached the house where she was staying. She pretended not to cry but her face was wet as she waved me goodbye, telling me it wouldn't be long before we'd be together again. I was a big boy and they don't cry, do they? They just ache inside.

Eventually the desperate billeting officers persuaded a Mrs Wilson to take me in on her firm instructions that it was only on a temporary basis. Unfortunately the night or two that Mrs Wilson had envisaged turned into weeks, and she started to make things awkward for me. She didn't like Brenda visiting and we had to part at the front gate. Having had my Dad taken away due to mental illness and my mother many miles away, I now felt I only had half a sister. The emotional cruelty Mrs Wilson and her family inflicted was just as bad as physical pain. As her messages to the billeting offices appeared to go unnoticed, she informed me that if I wasn't out of her house by that Friday, she would throw me out.

I managed to move in with Mrs Gallop (Auntie Annie) where my sister was living, but she didn't have the room so asked her lodgers, a couple, to foster me so I could remain with Brenda in the same house.

It wasn't long before Brenda noticed some marks on me and eventually I told her that the man had been hitting me with his leather belt. She informed Auntie Annie who didn't believe me, so she confronted the lodgers herself. They too denied it, but Brenda told everybody she saw including the village policeman, the Sunday school teacher, and the district nurse. Eventually a man with the title of 'Child Cruelty Officer' called. I had to show him the marks and he questioned the lodgers. Luckily he wasn't convinced of their story, and I was removed immediately from their care and placed with Auntie Annie. Fortunately they moved out.

We did return to Portsmouth for a holiday to visit our mother. Many of the evacuees who we had started out with had returned to the mainland. However, we came back to Wootton because it suited our mother as she was able to find work easily, the men having been called up. She did visit us once every six weeks and I remember this because that was when we were given egg and bacon for breakfast. She would bring us lots of nice things, like sweets and chocolate.

Wootton was a village that appeared not to have changed over the centuries. It was of unspoilt beauty. Although we could hear frequently the savage sounds of war and would watch the burning buildings a few miles away in Portsmouth and Southampton, we knew we were just the audience watching from a distance. Only one bomb fell near Wootton and that was probably unloaded by a German aircraft before returning empty across the English Channel.

Aunty Annie Gallop was a great influence during my early childhood and was a character I will always remember with great affection.

The house we lived in only had gas lighting on the ground floor. Candles were needed on all other floors. There was no problem sharing a bathroom because there wasn't one. A tin bath hung on a nail in the coal shed. The toilet was beyond the yard at the back of the house, sulking among the moss and ferns of a bygone age.

My sister made friends and eventually I had to make my own, but my one best friend Brenda was to leave me very suddenly. She died in hospital on 28 December 1941 from toxaemia. This was due to an infection she had picked up after a diphtheria inoculation at school. At the time this was given because diphtheria was a killer. We do not really know or ever will know what caused the infection. However, her death shook not only our family but the whole village. I will never forget the kindness the village showed me when she died. We had lived with Auntie Annie for two years and it was never going to be the same again. The last time I had seen Brenda was six weeks before she died, on her way to the doctors with her arm in a terrible state. I didn't wave to her but shouted some sarcastic comment about it not really hurting and that she was playing up. I now wish my last words to her had been different. My sister was eight years and ten months old when she died.

I had three main friends when I was evacuated: Hugh, Cyril, and David. Of the three I suppose Cyril was the one who showed me the ways of the countryside, but I also hold fond memories of the other two. They all made my childhood at Wootten an experience I will never forget.

I suppose being an evacuee on the Isle of Wight protected me from some of the horrors and hardships of war, like the Blitz and rationing. But I do remember some of the terrible things that occurred due to the war. There was a bomb that fell on the farm cottages that killed so many children. I also recall the face of a young soldier returning to the village after Dunkirk, and the kindness of American and Canadian soldiers with strange names like Marvin and Hank, who taught us to play basketball, and gave us gum and candy. Then one night in June they disappeared, we heard, to land on a strange beach in France.

I eventually returned to Portsmouth in 1946. The city was in ruins and large areas had been demolished by either bombing or for safety reasons. Fortunately there wasn't any damage to the houses where I lived. As I had left when I was young, I had to learn the layout of the streets. I was a virtual stranger in my own city due to the time spent away. It also had a bearing on the relationship I had with my mother. She hardly knew me and missed the freedom she had enjoyed. She also, in her worst times, resented me for being alive instead of my sister, which doesn't make for a good relationship.

So many children suffered due to wartime evacuation, but I was never happier than when I lived as an evacuee at Wootton Bridge, Isle of Wight, where for a while I felt I was part of one big family.

In 1979, forty years after I was evacuated, I hesitantly knocked on the door of David, my wartime friend. When his wife answered the door, we stared at each other for a few moments before I was able to say … 'Can David come out to play?'

Frank Faircloth

I was born in 1927 and had a normal, enjoyable childhood until 1938. I lived in the coastal area of North-East Essex and my father had two shops, tailors and cleaners in Clacton and Frinton-on-Sea.

Between 1938 and 1939 worries began to creep in. On my visits to an aunt in London, her small back garden that once had been full of flowers was gone. In its place now stood an Anderson air-raid shelter in which we would play. Street newspaper vendors were calling out, 'Crisis and War!' Cigarette cards which we collected started showing pictures of air-raid precautions and how to tape and seal windows and doors to prevent gas entering. We were required to go to the village hall to be fitted with gas masks. The gas risk came not just from air but from sea attack. Air-raid drills commenced in schools and explanations on how to take cover.

War was declared on Sunday 3 September 1939 at 11 a.m. When we came out of church people were calling out, 'We are at War!' Within eight months our family of seven—father, mother, four sons, and grandfather—were split apart in all directions. My three brothers were already of military age and were called up; one in the RAF and two in the Army.

I remember one morning sitting at home writing, being off school that day, when suddenly things jumped up and off the table. We found out it was a sea mine that had drifted into Clacton Pier.

Around midnight on 20 April 1940, I was awakened by gunfire and a plane flying very low over the rooftops. It was a Heinkel mine-laying plane with mines on board that had been damaged by Harwich AA gun battery. It made several circles low over the recreation ground near us, believed to be trying to land, then out to sea for its final approach. As it came back it touched rooftops and crashed on houses before reaching the recreation ground. I heard the crash and froze in bed. There was about one minute of complete silence, then the explosion. I jumped out of the bed and opened the room door and found the ceiling had come down on the landing and there was a fire glowing through the window. Two people in a house nearby were killed and many injured: these were the first casualties of the Second World War on the British mainland.

I can recall one of the scariest moments of all during 1942. It was in a rural location between Colchester and Clacton during harvest time. After dark I went outside upon hearing the siren. Suddenly overhead lights appeared. The Germans had started fresh tactics, dropping parachute oil bombs to set cornfields and farms alight. This was more frightening than HE bombs as they came down slowly, flaming above one's head. The ones just above me drifted 1 mile away, setting fire to Elmstead Hall farm buildings. I was really scared, as there is nothing worse than fire coming down from the sky.

As the Allies advanced north through France, German doodlebugs were launched from sites in Holland and Belgium straight at our area. It was frightening seeing them come towards us, and we were relieved when they passed overhead. Then there was the arrival of the V2 rockets. At dawn, when the sky was clear, we could see the vapour trail when launched in the east. They came overhead but only a few fell in our area.

During the early part of the war, William Joyce, traitor to Britain, used to make frequent propaganda broadcasts from Germany to the UK. His upper-class accent earned him the nickname 'Lord Haw Haw'. He was hanged for treason in 1946. His strong broadcasts would cut across our normal wavelengths, warning us of spies among us and threatening invasion. To reinforce the threat of spies he would point out the knowledge he had. On one occasion he stated, the clock on a local works building was five minutes slow, and it was.

In June 1940, I was evacuated with my school and the adult population of the coastal region were moved inland due to the invasion threat. My dad's shops were closed as there wasn't anyone left for trade so he found employment in London. My mother and grandfather went separately to live with some relatives further inland. Some furniture was left in the house but the rest was stored with relatives and in outbuildings belonging to friends. Home was gone. Coastal towns were taken over by the Army and made 'no-go' areas.

Our destination from Pathfields Road Secondary School in Clacton was Brimscombe Polytechnic School, where we had to wait for placement with foster parents. It was quite late by the time another child and I were called. We were placed in temporary care with some other evacuees from Birmingham, but the next morning we were taken to a kind elderly couple, Mr and Mrs Baglin of Walls Quarry. Mr Baglin was a postman and I spent many a happy time with him on his rounds. A short while before I returned to Essex we were placed elsewhere in Burleigh, as Mrs Baglin wasn't in the best of health.

School was shared with the local children. We wrote letters home to our parents and the teachers played a brilliant role in ensuring our well-being.

Leisure time was spent walking, fossil hunting in the rocks, and—as many children did during wartime—searching for fragments of aircraft, labelling them as to where they were found and the date. We did not think of the dangers involved in visiting the sites of crashes; it was just part of our life at that time. I would sit and sketch countryside scenes, one of my favourite pastimes.

After arriving in Gloucestershire in June 1940 air-raids increased against Bristol and Gloucester Docks, and while in bed one night a stray AA shell hit the hillside above our roof. However, we were luckily given good protection in a Cotswold stone house built in to the very steep hillside.

The journey back to the outskirts of London during the November 1940 bombing was scary. My brother who was on leave from the Army collected me in his car. We made our way across country with no sign posts or anything to show our location, just in case the country was invaded. I hid under a blanket in the back seat of my brother's car, not that it would have given any protection from a direct hit. When we approached London it was dusk and the blackout. While getting out of the car for a break we heard the wail of the sirens. We made our way onto the North Circular, a road which my brother was familiar with, and we saw the sky light up with searchlights and flares dropped by the planes. We soon realised that London was the target that night. We were stopped by wardens as bombs had fallen ahead and we had to change direction; we headed for the countryside, leaving the glowing fires behind us. Our anxious parents were glad to see us even though it was very late.

On my return from the school evacuation, a kindly fruit farmer let Dad have an old farm cottage, albeit 'condemned', in which Dad, Mum, Granddad, and I got together again.

The next worry was that my two brothers who were in the Army were reported missing. They were last heard of leaving in a boat from Durban for Singapore. Nothing more was heard about them for eighteen months. Eventually we were notified that they were POWs in the Far East. They were held there for another two years until the atom bomb and then they were released.

Whereas they returned home I received my call-up papers, having turned eighteen, in December 1945. I was in the Army two-and-a-half years, which concluded my decade of war and military service.

During these darks times there were some more light-hearted moments; how true some of the *Dad's Army* programmes were. In our rural cottage we were not far from several 'decoys' to attract bombers and, in our case, the decoy for Colchester railway junction. To protect us we had a Morrison steel table shelter. As this was not easy for Grandad to get down into, he would sit in his chair with a cushion on his head and a small galvanised metal bath to cover him.

Dad became an air-raid warden, and one evening an American fighter plane made a forced landing in orchards a short way from ours. Dad donned his helmet, jumped on his bike, and went off to assist. The pilot stepped out of the plane unhurt, but Dad did not reach there; he became entangled in wires the plane had brought down. We got him home bleeding but patched him up and all was well.

These memories mean a lot to me. I feel nostalgic about the kindness shown to us by the foster parents and local people. I remember the beautiful scenery and the sight of the Spitfires and Hurricanes flying below in the valley and sweeping up over the hill. Unfortunately, many of those who were ten when war was declared were affected by a severely disrupted education and left school at fourteen. There were no normal teenage evenings out, and most of the enjoyable things and sports were closed down. We missed so much of a period meant for growing up.

43

Len Townsend

It was in September 1939 that my brother Bill and I were evacuated with the school. Mum had filled our haversacks with spare clothes and other belongings and we marched from school down to Bethnal Green Junction to catch a train. I was nine years old and my brother eleven. It is only now that I realise the responsibility he had of keeping an eye out for me. I thought we were going on holiday, not realising how long we would be away from home. I can recall the train journey but can't remember how we arrived in Pakenham where we were to stay. I do remember it was a hot day and we sat outside the village hall for someone to claim us.

Eventually Mr Pawsey arrived in a car and said we were to stay with him. He was the chauffeur to the Martin family who owned Nether Hall, one of the local gentry. The Collins brothers were to stay in the house next door, which I think must have been the gardener's.

We were educated by teachers who had come with us and our classes were split between the village hall and the hall adjoining the village pub. I was in the pub hall and Mr Schilling was in charge. Eventually Mr Schilling left and we were taught by Mr Dyer.

We only stayed with the Pawseys for a few months as Mrs Pawsey was in poor health and looking after us didn't improve that. We then moved to stay with the Feveyers. They had their own children and lived in a house at the top of the village. Although our own home wasn't much, this house had no gas or electricity. We had to use oil lamps for light and wood fires for heating and cooking. We had to get water from a pump in the yard for drinking and rain water from the water butt for washing. The pump had to be primed by tipping a bit of water into it before you could pump water out. If the pump froze as it sometimes did in winter or if it ran out of water, we would have to walk down to the village where there was another pump and bring back buckets of water from there. You can imagine how much water was left in the buckets once we'd carried it up to the house—most of it slopped over the top. We had an outside toilet with a bucket under the seat. One day I was playing in the garden when my foot went down into the ground and into an old bucket that had been buried. It must have been full when it was buried, as it really did stink.

This was the first time I'd been away from home so it was left to Bill to tell me that 'There isn't really a Father Christmas,' and that it was Mum and Dad who bought the presents we found in our stockings and this year it would arrive in a parcel. Although it was lovely unwrapping the presents sent from Mum, Dad, and Nanny, it wasn't like Christmas at home.

One of our jobs was to go up into the woods and collect firewood. We would collect it and tie it into 'faggots' and carry it back on our shoulders. We weren't overfed at our billet; the meals seemed dry and in every one there was a lump of plain suet pudding which if you didn't eat it, you wouldn't get any afters. It was like eating lumps of lead.

Bert Feveyer worked delivering coal and would take me with him to get me to move the sacks to the edge of the lorry. I was so skinny and small I could hardly move them. My knuckles would get skinned raw from the sacking. He then got called up and we didn't see him again.

I never seemed to be in favour with Mrs Feveyer. I could do little right and her son Kenny could do no wrong. He could play with our things but we couldn't play with his. He would raise the roof.

Mum and Nanny came to live in the village at the 'Lodge' for a while when the Blitz was bad in London. They would go into The Fox, the village pub, for a drink and the villagers thought it terrible as women never went into the public bar.

I also had a quarrel with another boy and we decided to fight it out in the field behind the vicarage. Just as we were ready to start, someone called my name. I looked round and he hit me just under my eye. I wouldn't fight anymore but had a magnificent black eye. I wouldn't visit Mum either, as I was too scared to go. Mr Dyer stood me in front of the class as an example of what happens if you start fighting. I can still feel where the boy hit me.

Village life was strange and quiet for children who were used to the bustle of the East End, but we found lots of new things to do. The only sign of war was when the Germans tried to bomb the sugar beet factory at Bury St Edmunds, 5 miles away. We could hear sirens in the distance and would go to the Morrison shelter under the living room table, but this only happened a couple of times.

Once, when Bill and I had returned to London for a holiday, a couple of stray fire bombs fell in some bushes near the village but did no real damage. The villagers thought this was horrendous; meanwhile, in London the Blitz was starting in earnest, with raids every night. We had to sleep in our clothes to be ready to dash to a shelter. Mrs Johns along the street had an Anderson shelter in the yard and we had to run along there.

One night when the siren went we ran through the house, dashing for the shelter when we heard some 'screaming bombs' coming down. We just stopped by the back door way until they had landed and gone off. They were a frightening weapon, designed to cause panic. They had things attached to the fins which made the screaming noise as they rushed through the air and they sounded as though they were landing in front of you.

We returned to the village and eventually had to move out of the Feveyers and into the vicarage. There were quite a few of us there: Mr 'Pop' and Mrs Douglas, the vicar and his wife, our headmaster Mr Dyer, the nanny, two maids (Joan and Edna), and us evacuees (Bill, me, and another lad called Jimmy from Spitalfields). We slept on camp beds in one room and we ate our meals in the kitchen, except Jimmy who had to eat in the dining room because he was a naughty boy. Jimmy's family didn't send him any clothes so we were made to give him some of ours. Our Mum went potty because she said it was enough of a struggle clothing the two of us.

In 1942 my brother Bill left Pakenham at fourteen years old and went to work in Wales. This just left me with Jimmy, so I started saving my pocket money to pay for my fare home. I didn't realise how homesick I was. It was making me nervy and insecure and has had an effect on me throughout my life. I eventually saved up the money and wrote home to say I could pay my own fare. Dad came and collected me.

In 1943 I had to start school again and make new friends, as the ones I knew before the war were either still away or at different schools. Air-raids continued during the night, so we still had to go to the shelters, although it wasn't as bad as when the Blitz was at its height. We either went to Bethnal Green Tube Station or to the surface shelter they had built outside our house.

I preferred the Tube as you could buy a baked potato under the railway bridge at the Salmon and Ball, or crisps in the shop in the station. It was also a lot warmer than the surface shelter. The surface shelter saved the lives of my parents though. They had heard the siren and were just going out of the front door when a German plane swooped down and started machine-gunning the street. They ran behind the wall of the shelter and the bullets went all along the pavement in front of the house. We were always told that if a bomb dropped close by you had to sit with your mouth open and then the blast wouldn't blow your eardrums apart. My Dad worked in the heavy rescue service and had to work on some horrible incidents including the one at Bethnal Green Tube, where 173 people were crushed to death. He had to help get the bodies out, which didn't help his nerves. Fortunately, all my family survived the war.

44

Jim Reeve

Under the table, down in the basement in the dark, I lay terrified on the cold, hard floor listening to the symphony of death as the bombs cascaded out of the night sky on London. My mother lay across my brother and Ime like a protective hen. At four years old the talk of war puzzled me, and I asked the question that had been on my mind since the bombing had started. 'What is war Mum?'

She kissed my head. 'It's like you and Billy when you want something of his and he won't give it to you. What do you do? Fight. Countries are like that.'

My Aunt Milly piped up that my Mum should get us inoculated. Mum had laughed and corrected her that she meant evacuated. My aunt always got it wrong.

Another explosion made me curl up in a ball under Mum and I heard the implosion of glass as the house rocked and lumps of plaster shattered onto the floor, sending up a cloud of dust.

Shivering with fear I lay there as Billy, my three-year-old brother, started to scream and I remember my mother trying to calm him. Suddenly a noise filled the air with one continuous note. It was the sound we would welcome after a raid. The all-clear.

Mum struggled out from under the table taking Billy in her arms, while I held my aunt's hand. Wondering what it was like upstairs we picked out way through the glass and plaster, climbing the stairs to the next floor. It was then that I noticed the front door hanging as though clinging on by one hand. An air-raid warden poked his head round the door and asked if we were alright. We all answered that we were.

The kitchen appeared to have escaped any damage. Mum wanted to make a cup of tea and as my aunt said she couldn't smell any gas, on went the kettle. We were soon sipping sweet tea, seemingly the cure for everything. We then ventured upstairs to the bedrooms. As Mum entered my bedroom she let out a squeal and pointed to a great slab of concrete which lay across my bed. Lucky for us we were sheltering in the basement.

Later a workman came and repaired the front door while we helped clear up the rubble and glass. It wasn't long though before Mum had put us in the large pram and was pushing us down the street, saying that she was going to get us away. Most of the children had already been evacuated just after war was declared, but Mum always hoped the bombing would never happen.

When Mum arrived at the office building we were shown in and I was asked where I would like to go, the country or the seaside? I said the seaside, although I had no idea what it was going to be like. All I knew was it would be exciting.

Each night for the next fortnight Mum took us to the Underground station to sleep. Deep underground on the platform there were tiers of crowded beds stacked against walls with the overflow of people lying on the cold platform floor, leaving just enough room for passengers to get past. The smell of sweat and unwashed bodies made me heave. Sometime later after we had been evacuated a bomb dropped on the Angel Islington, the station we used, and over 100 were killed in the panic.

Each day Mum would rush us home to see if a letter had arrived from the council to tell us where we would be going. One day she held up a letter and announced that we would be going to Newquay on the Saturday, and that she was coming with us because my brother was so young.

My father was in Egypt so we never knew when we were going to see him again. My last memory of him was the roughness of his Army uniform as he picked me up and told me to look after Mum for him.

Early on the Saturday morning we trooped down to the station while other children and their parents joined us. Each child was struggling with their battered suitcase or paper carrier bag containing their belongings plus a packet of sandwiches and a bottle of cold tea. Every child had a label pinned to their lapel and, most importantly, round each neck hung a gas mask.

As I entered the station I stopped and stared in horror at the sight of the roaring monster who was about to take us to our destination.

It wasn't long before we left the streets of London and were swept out into the countryside. It was the journey of a lifetime, the first time we saw sheep, cows, pigs, and rabbits. Although I fell asleep the journey went on for hours. We passed unmarked stations with all their signs removed to confuse any German spies (or at least, that is what Mum told us).

Eventually we arrived in Newquay. I was so tired I could hardly walk and shuffled along to the awaiting single-decker bus. When we had arrived someone helped me down the steep steps and I looked up at the great hotel which stood out against the moonlit sky.

That night, twenty families sat at trestle tables eating carrots, mashed potatoes, and fish cakes. I still hate them, even now.

Next morning I work early and looked out of the window where I could see the sea swirling towards the hotel and crashing through the caves underneath us. I thought back to the nights in London under the table in the basement, listening to the bombs exploding. I was now safe and this was going to be the adventure of a lifetime.

45

Ugo Barella

I was born on 3 October 1937 in the small village of Garzeno, situated in a valley next to Lake Como, Northern Italy. I don't remember much of the beginning of the Second World War, being so young. Also living in such a remote place, the war didn't really seem to impact on us.

I lived with my parents, Aquilina and Pietro, and my siblings, Anacleto (born 1923), Rino (born 1930), and two sisters, Dorina (born 1925) and Rita (born 1928).

At the start of the war, Mussolini had asked all the women to give up their gold to buy arms. So as you can see, in Italy we didn't feel the true impact that people were experiencing elsewhere like France, Belgium, and Britain. I suppose you could say we went about our business without too much affect.

However, in 1942, this was about to change. My older brother was called up into the Italian Army as part of his national service and had been sent to work in Germany. Around this time there was utter confusion in Italy. Mussolini had been put in power by Hitler as previously, when Germany had invaded, the King had run away. In 1942 Mussolini called an election thinking he would again retain his position of power. He was wrong. He lost the election, because the Italians didn't really know who they should support.

When they decided to join the Allies, Hitler was not happy at all. My brother and lots of other Italians were then rounded up from their national service and sent to POW camps in Germany. Anacleto was taken to Buchenwald where he spent approximately three years working daily on a local farm. One night on returning to camp he tried to smuggle in a cabbage but was caught out; he was beaten and put in solitary confinement. He remained at the farm until he was released at the end of the war.

It was a while before we knew exactly where he had been taken. Information finally found its way to us as other local people also had sons who were sent there. So at least we had messages coming through. We were all very worried and all the families were relying on each other to hear from their sons. Letters were difficult to get through and would have been censored. But the communication network in the villages was excellent and, as I mentioned before, the church community and priests were pivotal within this communication network.

Mussolini went into hiding; speculation was that he was going to make his way across the mountains to the Swiss border and then into Germany.

Garzeno, being high up and backing onto hills that led to the mountains and on to Switzerland, was well-known as bandit country. Partisans operated in these areas but they were illiterate. It came to light a long time after the war that in November or December the British had dropped leaflets and a radio transmitter into the mountain forests hoping to alert the partisans and thereby enable communications with the Allies. However, the snow during these months makes the area quite impassable and it appears that the leaflets and transmitter were covered by the snowfall. They were found the following summer when the local farmers were taking their animals up for summer grazing. By then the war had ended some months before.

Around 3,000 people lived in the Garzeno area; many were quite poor and lived very basic lives. We were all self-sufficient and utilised the resources we had to survive. We had two cows and some chickens, and grew our own vegetables.

One day I remember very vividly. It was during the last days of the war. The church bells rang out loudly. It was well-known that they were used, especially in wartime, to bring the villagers out of their homes and for them to congregate in the square outside the church.

On this particular occasion we were all greeted by German officers. They separated us all. The women and children were sent into the church and the men to the school. The Germans were searching the village for a very important Italian general who was called Bianchini Bernardo. He had fled the Army when Hitler invaded Italy as he did not want to fight for the Germans; he had disbanded his regiment and disappeared. Most of his men would have joined the Resistance. He had fought in the First World War and continued in the military as a career. He came from Garzeno and his family were still there. He and his wife subsequently hid in the family home for over a year and the only people to know this were his family and the priest.

The Germans automatically assumed Bernardo would eventually return to his family home and village to take refuge. The general and the priest had already planned for such a search and had prepared a tomb in the cemetery for him to hide in. On the morning of the search they did not have time to put the plan into action, as they may have been seen by the Germans or by the villagers willing to disclose his whereabouts in fear of their own lives. The only option was to hide in the church, inside the organ's lower chamber.

My father had been so worried about the Germans coming as they would often raid homes, marching in and taking anything they fancied. My father had a new pair of leather shoes made by someone in the village—his only pair of shoes. He was so concerned the Germans would take them that he hid them behind the wine barrel in the cellar. The villagers would hide cheese and salami as these were favourites of the Germans and, if taken, would leave the people with little or no food.

We all wondered what was going to happen as the Germans searched all the properties for the general, and while we were in the church they began searching in there too. The priest had to watch while they checked with torches in the large organ. The Germans threatened that if they found the general anywhere in the village and the people had lied to say he wasn't there, they would burn the village to the ground.

There were a couple of Germans standing waiting while the search was going on. There were a few of us children and we were curious about their guns. The children in England had a bad image of Germans, but these two Germans let us village children look at their guns.

After the Germans were satisfied they couldn't find Bernardo they left. Fortunately for my father, the Germans didn't find his valuable shoes.

A few days later, Mussolini, his mistress Clara Petacci, and his henchmen were caught at the bottom of the valley in the town of Aquaseria, which is on the main road through to Switzerland along the side of Lake Como. They were taken to the piazza in Dongo and that night, in the absence of any local policing, to Germasino, a village above Dongo, to the barracks of the border guards ('Guardia di Finanaza') for security. The next morning they were taken down to the lake and to another village towards Como called Mezzegra, where they were executed on 28 April 1945. His fellow officers were shot against the railings in Piazza Dongo. You can still see the marks in the wall where the bullets hit. There is now a museum in Dongo housed in the building where it all took place.

When the war eventually ended my brother returned. We hadn't heard when he would be coming back, but the village grapevine had it that a group were about to board a train home. Apparently there was not enough room for them all and as they had just killed a cow, Anacleto decided he would stay and wait for the next train and enjoy the feast of fresh meat.

The village where we lived is still very quiet and the pace of life is wonderfully slow. The priest and church still hold a similar significance as that during the war, and some of the same families still live there.

Edith Rose Aitken-Smith

Aunt Rose's story and photos were passed to me many years ago when she wrote them down for me to keep with the family history. Unfortunately, Rose, her husband Arthur, and my cousin Peter have all since died. However, I felt it was of interest regarding the childcare arrangements of the time to put this short piece into these memories of the Second World War.

I was born in 1920, the fourth eldest of twelve children. In 1934 I started work at J. Lyons & Co Ltd., and eventually became a 'nippy' aged seventeen. At this time the Second World War hadn't been thought of and seeing as I was born in 1920, everyone was just getting over the first one. When the war started in 1939 I had to leave and go into war work. I first worked as a machinist sewing sailor's jackets and trousers, which was enjoyable. I had to leave after a year or so and go to the Royal Woolwich Arsenal on munitions.

When I married, I had moved to Greenwich and couldn't easily get transport to my previous work. I worked at the Arsenal until 1943 or '44, when my husband came home from the war medically unfit. As I then had to return to work I had to find childcare for our son. I had to put him in a wartime day nursery so I could earn extra money to pay the rent. We didn't need much for food as this was rationed and the ration books stated what we were entitled to. Life had to go on so we had to make the most of it.

We had to pay for Peter to attend the day nursery and we didn't get child allowance for the first child of the family. It cost 2s 6d a week for him to go there.

J. D. Ward

I arrived in Calverton by a roundabout route. I left Chingford with a number of other children on the 16 June 1940 heading for Stony Stratford on three red London buses. Our reception took place at the local junior school and was well organised. We were all issued with a card upon which were the details of our future foster parents. A local teacher then took us to the various locations. For some reason he detached me from the rest of the group and I was told to remain there until he came back. In fact, he vanished and I remained at the corner of Egmont Avenue/Claremont Avenue for a considerable time. Luckily two young ladies came past and guessed my situation. As per my card, they took me to the address, but I never actually saw these kind souls again.

I stayed at this billet for some months and attended Calverton School until several bombs were dropped at Upper Weald one Friday evening. The next day I and two other lads set off to Calverton to view the craters from a distance. When I arrived back at the billet there was a surprise waiting for me. My foster mother had developed pneumonia and was seriously ill. The billeting officer, a Mrs Roach, had been sent for and she had found me a new home, not in Stony Stratford but in Calverton at School House with a Mr and Mrs Tomkins, both of whom had disabilities but were the kindest and most cheerful of people.

The next day Mrs Roach walked me to Calverton and there we stood at the front door of School House. Mrs Tomkins soon answered; she had a round, kindly face and hair a mix of silver and gold. 'Come in, boy,' she said taking me in and removing my soaked clothes. Next she led me to the living room and a cheerful fire, with the faint scent of burning logs and flickering shadows on the walls.

From this moment my friendship with the Tomkins lasted for twenty-seven years until their passing. I have much to thank them for. And that is how I came to Calverton. Evening routine was always a pleasurable one with the choice of three games; cards, dominoes, or darts. At halftime, supper was laid out with large quantities of vegetables as Mr Tomkins cultivated his own. The star turn at supper had to be a Spanish onion, big as a man's fist and enough to set your throat on fire. I settled in well here.

At harvest time the village activity became intense. The mowing of different crops, wheat, barley, and oats would entice sizeable numbers of the villagers to follow the reaper for a free gathering by gleaning. This then found its way to privately kept fowl destined for Christmas.

The village fete took place about mid-summer either in the rectory back garden or the school should it be a rainy day. The takings went to the church funds. There were stalls and also sideshows for amusement. I remember at the shooting gallery, a pellet fired by an air rifle rebounded from the target and landed in the rector's mouth. Now and again a 'social' would be held in the school, where some refreshments and dancing were to be had.

When I first came to Calverton the local water was supplied by wells. School House had its own. There stood another well halfway through Lower Weald and supplied the Tomkins. Mr Tomkins collected water with the help of a yoke and two buckets every evening. About 1941 or 1942 mains water to the village was laid on by the council, and Mr Tomkins became one of the workmen involved. I used to visit him each day and loved to watch the progress of the pipe trench from Stony Stratford; also the laying of the pipes, some joined by rubber seals and steel washers, others by molten lead. The mains pipes were of about 4 inches in diameter.

Throughout my association with the village there was no pretence of a reasonable sewage system. A tank was pulled around the village by a poor old horse of Steptoe vintage. The operator stopped at each house, emptied the privy into his bucket, which then was transferred to the tank. The stench nearly knocked you over. On this day of the week the schoolchildren used to run for cover.

There were some war experiences at Calverton. Enemy aircraft were heard from time to time with their distinctive engine sound, a low moaning warble, on their way to bomb the Midlands. On 14 November 1940 my foster parents and I went to the cinema at Stony Stratford. At the end of the performance we emerged into the street to find an air-raid warning in progress. German aircraft could be heard above and they continued until the early morning. On our way home a glow could be seen in the sky to the north. It was the bombing of Coventry. The Tomkins made me a temporary bed downstairs that night under a table with cushions and blankets. They each slept in a chair at either end of the table for my protection. It was a frightening experience.

On another occasion the village was bombarded with incendiary bombs. They were heard during the night hitting the ground. Having assessed the situation we three headed towards the rectory with many other people and there were organised into fire-fighting parties. I joined with a Miss Taylor and between us we carried some sand in an old bath to the Leys, where we delivered it to the menfolk fighting the fires. Eventually when the incendiaries were either overcome or burned out we returned home and had a calming cup of tea. At this point I discovered that I had departed from the house in such a hurry that I had left my footwear off!

There were one or two preparations to combat an enemy invasion. In the island at the junction of the road to Beachampton a pit was dug, presumably an intended machine gun position. At the bottom of the hill to Middle Weald a large tree trunk had been installed, pivoted at one end and with a wagon wheel at the other. In the event of an invasion the trunk was to be pushed across the road to surprise any German troops proceeding apace down the hill. No doubt the Home Guard would have given the *coup de grâce*.

The last of the wartime activities was the building of two radio stations. Rumour had it that they were both connected with Bletchley. Maybe this was so.

The people who owned Calverton Place were quite generous to evacuees, allowing us the use of a field as a playground. Another time, we children were given a party on the lawn of Calverton Place. An egg-and-spoon race was modified into a potato-and-spoon race, eggs being short at that time. But the great treat of the day was a very large tub of ice cream, something we hadn't seen for years. Finally, every child was given a half crown. One tends to remember things like this. I believe that the family who did this for us was Bowater.

I joined the church choir in my early days at Calverton. This meant attending two services on Sundays and choir practise one evening in the week. The Reverend Raymond Bathurst Ravenscroft was the rector at the time; he was good company. In his own time he was a ghost-hunter and told many an eerie story. Mr Tomkins maintained the churchyard in good order and was also the sexton, stoking the fires up when necessary and ringing the bells on a Sunday. Sometimes I did this for him.

Returning home from my third evacuation place at Christmas 1942, air-raids were a fairly common thing, but I do not recall an excessive amount of bombing. Anti-aircraft gunfire created the most noise and it was advisable to head for the nearest air-raid shelter when the siren sounded. It was in our family shelter that I discovered a means of giving oneself a false sense of security by jamming a finger in each ear, which reduced the noise of the gunfire. Raids usually lasted about thirty to forty minutes. Sometimes they were repeated two or three times per night. Hence, sleep was often interrupted. One morning Mother and I were heading for a bus stop at North Chingford and were caught out in an air-raid. Gunfire was heard and seen while we ran the length of Pretoria Road to get some shelter. A delayed siren then sounded. In the sky were the objects of the AA fire, two German aircraft, shining silver in the sun's reflection and with contrails showing, turning for home. Years later in connection with work I obtained a large map showing some of Essex and the Thames Valley and managed to plot the above course of those aircraft. It seems they were looking for a well-known power station.

The advent of the V1 unmanned flying bomb gave a different dimension to the war. A V1 engine had a deep growl that stopped when the fuel ran out. It then flew on until it hit the ground and exploded. The V2 was a rocket launched, like the V1, from German-held territory. It rose vertically for about 70 miles and then dropped on to its target—England. It carried about the same amount of explosive as the V1. Blast from both weapons could be devastating. The V2 had a silent approach, being supersonic. It sounded like a tremendous clap of thunder following the explosion.

According to *Chingford at War*, the first two V2s fell on the country on 8 September 1944: one at Chiswick, the other at Parnham Wood near Epping.

At 2 a.m. on 5 February 1945, the front door of our home in Goldsborough Crescent, Chingford, was blown off by the V2 that fell in Endlebury Road. On my way to school that morning I passed immediately by the site and was shocked by the devastation.

All things come to an end, so they say, as did the war in Europe. On VE-Day, 8 May 1945, I travelled with Mother to central London to watch the celebrations. There were masses of people everywhere, singing, shouting, dancing, climbing lamp standards, blocking Piccadilly Circus, and holding up our bus to an inch-by-inch crawl. We eventually arrived in front of Buckingham Palace with tens of thousands of other people and watched as the royal family waved to the crowds. We also saw Winston Churchill leave for the BBC to make his historic announcement. This was, if I remember rightly, 'The end of the war will take place at one minute past midnight tonight. But in the interest of saving lives the ceasefire has already been sent down the line.'

On our homeward bus a Canadian soldier entertained us by climbing the platform handrail and clinging there, monkey-like, while his girlfriend tried to pull him down. No luck, he was plastered.

The war in the Far East continued for about another three months. During this time a young airman who lived opposite us in Goldsborough Crescent was captured by the Japanese and tortured for information, but he did not give any away. He was then murdered. He later received the George Cross posthumously.

I did not see any celebrations at the end of this part of the war as I was camping with my old friends from Calverton choir.

48

Pamela Drummond (née Taylor)

When the Second World War started I was seven-and-a-half years old. The exact date of our first evacuation is unclear, but at the time we were in Sittingbourne so I am sure it was more than likely 1 September 1939. We had been sent there as an early evacuation, so weren't at our home in Chatham when war was declared.

My school was St John's Infant School and I was due to start big girl's school at the beginning of the autumn term. Due to the war this didn't happen.

My ten-year-old cousin, Hazel Strong, was with me. We were marched in lines from school to Chatham Railway Station, where we were transported to Sittingbourne. When we arrived, carrying our minimal belongings, we walked the streets with our teachers who were trying to find billets for us all.

Hazel and I were left at a house in Spring Street. The woman reminded me of a witch. We were shown into a very small, dark living room. Arranged on the table covered by a green baize cloth was a selection of playing cards. On the floor was a semi-circle of ash. The woman had been pipe smoking and while sitting at the table playing patience had been knocking the ash out onto the floor. She quickly put all our emergency rations into a small wall cupboard in one corner of the room. On the big black range stood two black saucepans, spitting and hissing liquid over the stove. They reminded me of cauldrons. Below the range was the ubiquitous black cat curled up on a rag rug. The image was complete.

Fortunately for us we only stayed one night at this billet. The experience was far from pleasant and we left there with numerous flea bites and desperately hungry, as we hadn't been given any food. When we'd asked at breakfast for something to eat the woman gave us a ha'penny and told us to get some chewing gum from the machine up the road. Luckily we remembered the leftover sandwiches from the journey the day before. As they were banana they hadn't faired particularly well in the haversack overnight.

On the second day we were moved to another billet. We weren't a pretty picture as we were rather unkempt not able to wash. I was, by now, covered in daubs of 'blue bag' put on to relieve the flea bites. The next billet was clean, but we had to share the toilet and it was situated down the garden.

Although we could only attend Milton Regis School for half-days we were not allowed to return to the house until 4.30 p.m. each afternoon, even if the weather was bad. Although we were fed and watered by this lady we were certainly not shown any affection. If we saw her while we were out she would completely ignore us.

Sometime in the following June I caught measles. I was sent to a big house on the hill above Sittingbourne, especially for evacuees. While I was there Hazel was evacuated again, but farther afield, to South Wales. It wasn't long before I too found myself on another train full of children on our way to Wales. On reaching Cardiff I thought I would be reunited with Hazel, however I was made to stay on the train. I can remember crying and fighting because I was sure I had been told Hazel would be there to meet me and she wasn't. We arrived very hot and very tired in Neath and were then ushered aboard a charabanc to our final destination, Pontardawe.

My time in Pontardawe was a complete contrast to Sittingbourne. My new 'Auntie Mabel' was a very kind lady. Although very strict, as I wasn't allowed out to play with the other children, I still felt reasonably content. Her husband, 'Uncle Willie', was a lovely man and bought me the Beano comic. Hazel was able to visit during Christmas of 1940. It was an unhappy time for her as her mother had been killed by a land mine and her father was already dead. Thankfully Auntie Mabel let Hazel stay. She took her under her wing and I was overjoyed. We both had a good time in Pontardawe despite causing various problems. I needed to be prescribed spectacles as my eyes were playing up; I had to have my milk teeth removed by the dentist so that the new teeth could grow down; and lastly my tonsils needed to be removed, which required a visit to Swansea Hospital during a very scary air-raid. I will always remember Auntie Mabel taking me all the way back home in a taxi and giving me barley sugar to suck. Then poor Hazel scaled her leg badly and also fell down a metal spiral staircase at Uncle Willie's shop. They definitely had their hands full with the pair of us. Auntie Mable was so very good and kind, despite, as I later realised, being no spring chicken by then.

In 1942 we returned to Chatham just as the V1s started because our English teachers who had accompanied us to Wales were recalled. The only other option was for us to remain in Wales and be taught in Welsh. My memory of education in Wales was of the nature rambles we had on the mountainside and of Wednesday and Friday afternoons when our beloved teacher Mrs Tasker would read a chapter of *Wind in the Willows*— sheer bliss.

During the war we would always wear hand-me-downs. Mum would unpick jumpers and re-knit with the wool. We shared beds, sometimes top and bottom. A favourite food was bread and dripping, and because I was used to dried eggs, when we eventually had fresh eggs back again I didn't know how to use them and had to ask. I remember Mum would make cakes with cod liver oil to save on the fat. They tasted quite reasonable and actually rose up.

I was very proud of Father, as he was in the Royal Navy and had just completed thirty-two years of service. He had to go back in for the duration of the war but was awarded the Distinguished Service Medal for service work. The war did cause us to lose some of our distant family.

49

Gordon Carter

At the start of the Second World War I was aged seven. When we heard the announcement on the wireless my mother was very concerned, as my father was severely disabled from the First World War.

We lived in a terraced house split into two flats. My parents had one bedroom and my brother and I shared the other. We lived close to Hampstead Heath, which was eventually covered by gun batteries and balloons as it was on a direct flight path into the City of London.

We had a damp Anderson shelter in the small back garden, but it was never used. My friends and I pretended it was a submarine. My father worked in the Handley Page factory which was building bombers. At night he was a fire warden on the top of a local building. The majority of my school was evacuated but my mother decided that if we were going to die, we would all go together.

I had joined my church choir at six years old, my brother already being head boy. Soon we were the only boys in the choir and my mother was one of the few people in the congregation. By 1943 I was one of the few remaining choristers in London, singing at weddings, hospitals, in shelters, and sadly at many funerals. I was invited to join the St Paul's Cathedral and Westminster Special Choir to perform on the special occasions. My final service was to lead the choir in front of Princess Elizabeth. I was also asked if I would like to climb to the top of St Paul's Cathedral under the gold ball of the cross, 365 feet high. At the time it was the tallest building in London. I was thrilled. The last 12 feet were up a ladder to the windows which had been completely destroyed by bomb blast. All around St Paul's was flattened and the empty spaces filled by enormous water tanks used to fight the fires.

Although I was travelling all over London, my mother always said, 'Don't worry, you will always be safe in God's house.' Most church walls were very much thicker than street shelters. We cleared out our coal cellar and sat in there playing cards or singing. Across the road from our home was a large block of flats and underneath there was shops. During the heavy bombing which lasted around seventy days, my aunt and uncle were bombed out and came to stay with us.

During the bombing all our windows were shattered and the ceilings came down. Less than 100 yards away, two houses were completely destroyed.

Clothes were rationed but were too expensive, so we wore hand-me-downs jumble sale items. The Admiralty took over our school so we met a teacher in a house for a few days a week.

As children we found life scary, exciting and adventurous, hunting for pieces of shrapnel.

I also recall a friend of mine inviting me into his flat. In his bedroom he had this German bomb hanging from his ceiling. His father was a bomb disposal NCO.

The final stages of the war came as I had passed my scholarship to go to grammar school. This coincided with the doodlebugs and V2 rockets.

Around 1943 I had to have my tonsils and adenoids removed so my mother took me to the hospital (with my gas mask). When I reached the ward I found the windows were protected on the outside by sandbags to about a foot from the top. At night we could see the searchlights lighting up the sky through the small gap in at the top. At the end of the week they asked me if I had ever had ear problems and I told a little lie and said no, so they released me. I was lucky, for the ward had a direct hit a few days after I left.

Food being scarce, bread and dripping was quite popular. I used to have a slice when I got home from school with a little salt on it. In the park I mentioned was a large orchard and during the fruit season my mother would get me up early and we would walk to the park about 6 a.m. just as the park keeper was opening up and if it had been a wet and windy night there would be lots of windfalls of apples and pears. I would run around filling up our baskets. This would keep us fed with apple pies and stewed pears for some time.

In 1944 my brother went off to join the Army, eventually landing in Italy and going on to Germany. When he was demobbed he brought me home a box full of 48 Fry's cream bars. He had save up all his sweet coupons to buy them.

My wife was evacuated with her brother when she was five. She was sent to Cartmel near the Lake District, which was a very long journey from London in the wartime. She stayed in a small cottage with an elderly couple who were very kind but very strict. My wife described all the details of the cottage and school to me, and a few years ago I decided to take her there.

Nothing had changed; the cottage and the school were exactly how she'd described them. In the garden of the cottage was an elderly gentleman and I told him about my wife. He asked us in to meet his wife, who showed my wife all over the cottage; apart from the kitchen, it had not been altered. We sat and had tea and talked about those days.

50

Barbara Harvey

I was born in Colchester on 17 April 1939, so I imagine I was about five to six months old when war broke out. My father was then twenty six and was whisked away by the Army until he was demobbed on 20 January 1946.

My memories seem to lock in when I was about three-and-a-half. I vaguely remember this soldier (my father) coming home in uniform. He was only home for a very short time. My mother and I were sharing a house with my aunt, uncle, and cousin so we had limited space and I had to share a bed with Mum. The night Dad returned I had to sleep on the floor; nine months later my little brother was born, on 17 December 1943.

During the time that my mother was pregnant, I remember being woken many times and put into a metal shelter in the sitting room with my cousin. One night is still very clear in my mind. My mother's younger sister was visiting when the siren sounded. She and Mum dragged the mattress and us children downstairs, tucked us up in the shelter, then proceeded to pace up and down the room. I watched and listened. I could see two pairs of legs and heard their voices. My aunt was saying, 'I must get home to Mum and Dad.' My Mum sounded very worried and advised her to wait for the all-clear. She would not and I then heard my Mum say to her, 'You must throw yourself flat on the ground if you hear anything coming.'

Somehow my father was home for the birth of my brother. I was woken by my aunt to come and see this tiny little black-haired, blue-faced yelling bundle, and again caught a glimpse of my soldier father.

The only other occasion I remember was when Dad came home bringing a tin with some boiled sweets in it. I had never tasted sweets before and was told off for being greedy!

I have a great feeling of nostalgia when I hear Vera Lynn or any wartime music because it takes me back to a time when, although we were poor and had very little, people were friendly and pulled together to make life bearable.

I had started school before the war ended and clearly remember the siren going and being made to walk close to the wall to get to the shelter in the playground. We then had to sing 'ten green bottles' as loudly as possible, presumably to block out the sound of aircraft flying over.

I was almost seven when my father came home for good. It took a long time for me to accept this stranger in my life and who seemed to take my mother's attention away from me.

It was only in the latter part of my father's life that he spoke of his experiences during the war; for many years he never mentioned it at all. I felt sadness as I looked into his eyes and thought of the seven years of his love, youth, and strength that I had missed. I felt so angry, but I was fortunate he came home when many did not.

I am now seventy-five and much water has passed under the bridge. While tidying out my parents' home I kept finding things that made me realise how little we knew of my father's time in the war and how many bits and pieces he had kept: letters he sent home, service records, and demob papers.

All my memories and emotions which have made up my life have surfaced again, happy and sad. As a family we had many good years after my father came home; we became a strong, caring unit. It was then that I realised what a clever and wise man he was.

51

Pam & Terry Woods

Our war experience started when we were bombed out of our home in Leytonstone and moved to Ilford. When war started in 1939 Pam was one and I was four. It wasn't long before things changed yet again.

Our evacuation journey during the summer of 1944 was over 100 miles away and most certainly the furthest that we had ever travelled. On the train we ate some of the food Mum had prepared and I must admit to disgracing myself by squirting the man on the seat next to me with tomato pips. After travelling most of the day we eventually arrived exhausted, at the home of Mr and Mrs Green, who lived in a small village called Bucklebury, near Thatcham.

The contrast between the devastation and dejected atmosphere that prevailed in town centres and public places and the oasis of calm and long forgotten normality that we had come to was very noticeable, even to us children. All around us were buildings and people untouched by the war, who spoke with strange accents and had so much space around them. The sun seemed extra warm and welcoming to us, with miles of common and fields for Pam and me to play in. We could not have imagined anything better.

Horace Green was a tall, thin, old looking man who seemed to have a constantly mournful expression on his face. He mostly dressed in striped trousers with a black waistcoat and a black jacket over it.

We later found out that he was the local undertaker so that probably accounts for his perpetual and generally sad demeanour. His wife was also fairly tall and thin, her hair set permanently in a tight bun at the back of her head. Whatever the day she had sleeves down to her wrists and buttoned, and wore a long pinafore.

Mr and Mrs Green had two daughters about the same age as Pam and me, and although we felt shy during our first meeting with them, we all got on quite well. I remember that they seemed to be in a constant fit of giggles whenever we spoke, telling us that we 'spoke funny', making us repeat words again and again until Pam and I eventually lapsed into embarrassed silence.

Mum having seen the room that we were to live in and satisfied with it then started her long return journey home to Dad; it must have been awful for her not knowing when or if she would ever see us again. I remember that Pam and I cried a lot when she left. We felt so alone in this strange environment and couldn't really understand why we were there. If Mum and Dad were going to continue to live in our house in Ilford, then we felt that we should be there with them.

We did not feel angry at being left there, just very sad that Mum and Dad were not with us. The Green family lived in a very small hamlet of about ten bungalows and three farms; just across the lane to their bungalow there was a really big common, which appeared to stretch away as far as the eye could see.

The Greens' bungalow had a front garden with a thorny hedge that divided it from the lane. I remember that the front garden was mostly lawn with some roses around the sides; the back garden, however, had a small shed and seemingly endless rows of vegetables with lines of canes for bean plants and some shed-like buildings which housed their chickens. Right at the end of the garden was an earth toilet in a small brick building with a tiled roof, the inside of this building was covered with spiders' webs. Not a place to sit around in for very long unless one was desperate.

In the back garden was also a well that supplied the water for the bungalow. Due to its location, the village did not have any mains water provision, so all water used in the bungalow had to be pumped up by hand from the well. This meant a fairly rigid regime of programming for preparation of meals, washing, baths, or using the special indoor toilet. The Greens were very proud of their indoor toilet. We later found out it was used for special occasions only, when they had visitors and wanted to show off their new facility. Normally the toilet at the end of the garden was the one used on a day-to-day basis; this took a lot of getting used to. Pam and I not being accustomed to water conservation quite often inadvertently emptied the small internal water tank by using the special indoor toilet just as Mrs Green would be about to prepare the evening meal or do some clothes washing. So, if we wanted to use the toilet we had to first prepare by with furious hand-pumping to top up the small tank; only then could we use the toilet.

With the Greens not having a car to take us to school and no bus service available we had to walk to school across the common. This was a distance of 3 to 4 miles door to door. I am sure that Mum would have been upset if she had realised that we were making this journey twice a day by ourselves. She would have been even more upset if she knew we used to stop off at a wood turner's hut in the middle of the common at Turners Green to watch him at work on his lathe.

The school that we attended was in a partially converted church hall and consisted of two classes. One class catered for children up to eleven and the other for older children up to fifteen. The division between the two classes was a screen made from old doors fixed together which stretched across the hall from side to side. It swayed with quite ominous creaking in a most alarming fashion every time that an outside door was opened and one of the teachers would rush to put her back to the screen to stop it falling over. Lengths of wood were later fixed to each side to brace the screen and the swaying was greatly reduced. It still creaked when a door was opened and the class looked around very apprehensively, worried about it all falling down.

The school toilets were completely open to the elements and public gaze, and like the Greens' toilet it was a place that you went only if you were really desperate. If you asked permission to use the toilet, a teacher would go out with you and make sure that you washed your hands in a bucket of cold water left in the small yard that also served as a playground.

At dinner times we would all be marched outside to wash our hands in the same bucket of cold water. After we had eaten we would all line up to wash our hands and faces, again in the same bucket of cold water—some hygiene.

The dinners most days were dreadful, largely boiled potatoes and corned beef or cabbage. We always carefully turned over the potatoes to remove the earwigs that had been cooked inside them. It is no wonder that we tried to eat from the hedges on our way into school or on the way home afterwards.

The ladies serving out our dinners used to dismiss the earwigs by telling us we were lucky to have extra 'meat' with our meal. Needless to say we soon removed the offending insects from our food. They told us off when they saw us doing this, saying that we should eat the earwigs as they'd only eaten the same potato that we had on our plates.

52

Stanley Parker-Ross

I wasn't among the initial exodus of evacuees who left at the outbreak of the war. I followed in June 1940. I was just ten.

Castle Cary in Somerset was our ultimate destination, where we were assembled in a school hall close to the station. It was here, while seated cross-legged on the floor that we waited to be 'chosen' by prospective foster parents.

It was an elderly lady who was brave enough to select me and two other boys of a similar age. I learned later that she was Mabel Gould, a Christian spinster in her early sixties who played the organ at the local church. She drove us in her tiny old Austin car back to her sizable cottage in Hornblotton, a quaint stone building dating back to the eighteenth century. After being generously allotted a bedroom each, we were given refreshments. Before she allowed us to do anything else, we were required to write a letter home to our respective parents.

One might conclude that the cottage was quite modern, bearing in mind its era, but the running water with which it was served came through pipes in such an ill state of repair that the taps had to be left fully open over bowls to make use of the meagre trickle of water. The single water closet was taboo to all but guests. We boys were obliged to use a chemical toilet which, during that hot summer, was anything but fragrant. No electricity of course, but a battery-driven wireless was used just once each evening at nine to bring our host up-to-date with the war news.

Thus began a life totally alien to anything any of us had experienced. It stood in sharp contrast to life in the lower working-class slum in the East End, in which we'd been born and spent our formative years. The house was surrounded by an acre or so of land on which the old lady kept a single cow and around fifty hens.

I did notice some antipathy to our presence from the scant population, which troubled me at the time. It seemed that London youths were capable only of leaving gates open, stealing fruit from the numerous orchards, and, of course, creating havoc in the process. No doubt there was some truth in this. Fortunately some allowance was made by more liberal neighbours for the fact that these children had been torn from their native habitat and for the most part were bewildered and unhappy.

Mostly I remember the old lady's kindness. As I had a penchant for unsweetened tea, whenever it was served at meals she would take the trouble to provide a separate jug solely for me. At a time when food was short, she would nonetheless ask if we objected to meat paste for the sandwiches that she packed each day, along with a bottle of her homemade elderflower cordial for school lunch.

Schooling was to be the biggest problem. There was just one tiny infants' school in Lovington, a hamlet just a mile away. We did attend there for a while, sitting at desks far too small, alongside five-year-olds. The only secondary school which we attended later involved a walk of some 6 miles.

I vainly attempted to expand my education by studying an ancient copy of *The Encyclopædia Britannica* which I'd discovered among an eclectic assortment of books in one of the rooms.

My stay in the West Country, enjoying a healthy lifestyle and safe from the Blitz, came to an end quite suddenly when my mother, who had come to stay for a short holiday, decided I must come home.

Apart from falling bombs the education problem was even worse in London. The role of the rambling old Victorian school had been extended during the war, from its original function for infants and juniors, to accommodate all children up to the normal leaving age (then fourteen).

Staffing was a problem of course. Naturally, the majority of able-bodied men had been conscripted into the armed forces and we were left with the elderly, infirm, and often incompetent. Classes had become so large that it was impractical to pack the youngsters into single classrooms. Instead, a compromise was reached whereby pupils were accommodated in morning and afternoon shifts, alternating each week.

For most, time was spent roaming the streets, exploring bombed buildings, and sabotaging the war effort by vandalising the neighbourhood, while others, like me, attempted to fill the educational void at the local library.

The Blitz was of course a problem. Most children had to sleep in the damp, stifling atmosphere of an Anderson or other type of shelter with the irrational but comforting philosophy that only others got bombed.

The war was still raging when, at fourteen, I substituted full-time education for evening classes. It was the summer of 1944. With an acute labour shortage, it wasn't difficult to get work—even if the employers were taking advantage of the cheap and plentiful teen labour.

Officially no longer a child, my story should now end. Did I ever revisit my temporary home? Yes! I saw again the old house with the fields of wheat waving in the breeze. I attended a communion service at the tiny church and finally visited the modest grave of Mabel Gould, who had had such an impact on my life.